# Sacred North-East Scotland

SACRED PLACES SERIES

# Sacred
# North-East Scotland

## SCOTLAND'S CHURCHES SCHEME

SAINT ANDREW PRESS
Edinburgh

First published in 2010 by
SAINT ANDREW PRESS
121 George Street
Edinburgh EH2 4YN

ISBN 978 0 7152 0944 8

**British Library Cataloguing in Publication Data**
A catalogue record for this book is available from the British Library.

Typeset in Enigma by Waverley Typesetters, Warham, Norfolk
Manufactured in Great Britain by Bell & Bain Ltd, Glasgow

BUCKINGHAM PALACE

As Patron of Scotland's Churches Scheme, I warmly welcome this publication as part of the *Sacred Places* series of books being produced by the Scheme.

The story of the heritage and culture of Scotland would be lacking significantly without a strong focus on its churches and sacred sites. I am sure that this guidebook will be a source of information and enjoyment both to the people of Scotland and to our visitors.

Anne

# Scotland's Churches Scheme

*www.sacredscotland.org.uk*

Scotland's Churches Scheme is an ecumenical charitable trust, providing an opportunity to access the nation's living heritage of faith by assisting the 'living' churches in membership to:

- Promote spiritual understanding by enabling the public to appreciate all buildings designed for worship and active as living churches
- Work together with others to make the Church the focus of the community
- Open their doors with a welcoming presence
- Tell the story of the building (however old or new), its purpose and heritage (artistic, architectural and historical)
- Provide information for visitors, young and old

The Scheme has grown rapidly since its inception in 1994, and there are now more than 1,200 churches in membership. These churches are spread across Scotland and across the denominations.

The *Sacred Scotland* theme promoted by Scotland's Churches Scheme focuses on the wish of both visitors and local communities to be able to access our wonderful range of church buildings in a meaningful way, whether the visit be occasioned by spiritual or heritage motivation or both. The Scheme can advise and assist member churches on visitor welcome, and, with its range of 'how-to' brochures, provide information on research, presentation, security and other live issues. The Scheme, with its network of local representatives, encourages the opening of doors and the care of tourists and locals alike, and offers specific services such as the provision of grants for organ-playing.

*Sacred Scotland* (www.sacredscotland.org.uk), the website of Scotland's Churches Scheme, opens the door to Scotland's story by exploring living traditions of faith in city, town, village and island across the country.

The site is a portal to access information on Scotland's churches of all denominations and is a starting point for your special journeys.

We are delighted to be working with Saint Andrew Press in the publication of this series of regional guides to Scotland's churches. In 2009, the first three volumes were published – *Sacred South-West Scotland*; *Sacred Fife and the Forth Valley*; and *Sacred Edinburgh and Midlothian*. This volume, *Sacred North-East Scotland*, is one of three being published in 2010 (the others are *Sacred Glasgow and the Clyde Valley* and *Sacred Borders and East Lothian*), to be followed by a further three books in 2011, when the whole country will have been covered. We are grateful to the authors of the introductory articles, Professor John Hume, one of our Trustees, and Henry R. Sefton, for their expert contributions to our understanding of sacred places.

The growth of 'spiritual tourism' worldwide is reflected in the million-plus people who visit Scotland's religious sites annually. We hope that the information in this book will be useful in bringing alive the heritage as well as the ministry of welcome which our churches offer. In the words of our former President, Lady Marion Fraser: 'we all owe a deep debt of gratitude to the many people of vision who work hard and imaginatively to create a lasting and peaceful atmosphere which you will carry away with you as a special memory when you leave'.

Dr Brian Fraser
*Director*
Scotland's Churches Scheme
Dunedin
Holehouse Road
Eaglesham
Glasgow
G76 0JF

# Invitation to Pilgrimage
## North-East Scotland

In past days, going on a pilgrimage to North-East Scotland meant a long, arduous journey by road and ferry. Nowadays, access is much easier by road, rail and air. Robert Louis Stevenson asserted: 'To travel hopefully is a better thing than to arrive'. He travelled for travel's sake. Modern Christians think pilgrimage is all about arriving rather than travelling. Such an attitude would have deprived us of *The Canterbury Tales*. Sir Walter Ralegh thus described his preparations for pilgrimage:

> Give me my scallop-shell of quiet,
> My staff of faith to walk upon,
> My scrip of joy, immortal diet,
> My bottle of salvation,
> My gown of glory, hope's true gage,
> And thus I'll take my pilgrimage.

Recent excavations at the Kirk of St Nicholas in Aberdeen revealed four pilgrimage scallop-shells and a tiny pilgrim badge depicting the Pieta: the Virgin Mary and the dead Christ. The undercroft of St Nicholas Kirk is a Chapel of St Mary of Pity. Other dedications to St Mary in Aberdeen include St Mary of the Snows (the Snow Kirk in Old Aberdeen), St Mary in the Nativity (King's College Chapel) and St Mary of the Assumption (the Roman Catholic Cathedral).

Celtic monks were enthusiastic pilgrims, but their journeys took them not to sacred but to deserted places which they aimed to make sacred by driving out evil through prayer and fasting: St Palladius in Fordoun, St Ternan in Arbuthnott and Banchory, St Drostan at Deer, St Machar at Old Aberdeen. Some scholars assert that Machar is really Ninian and there are traces of St Ninian's activities all over the North-East.

As the pilgrim approaches Aberdeen from the south, a panorama of spires comes into view suggesting that this must be a holy city – what John

Knox would have described as a School of Christ. Knox found such a school in Geneva, but he would have been disappointed in Aberdeen, both then and now. Aberdeen was reluctant to accept the Protestant Reformation and was even more reluctant to accept the National Covenant of 1638. The North-East was also not too keen on the Presbyterian settlement of 1690. In modern times, Aberdeen has been described as the most secular city in Scotland. Why, then, so many spires?

The proliferation of churches in Aberdeen and other towns in the North-East is largely owing to ecclesiastical division and conflict. The Disruption of 1843 caused every minister in the city to 'come out' of the Church of Scotland and to abandon their churches and manses in favour of the newly established Free Church of Scotland. This meant an immediate doubling of churches, for each minister had a new church provided for him. The signs of this are still visible in the various pairs of churches often confronting each other, the parish church on one side of the street and the Free church on the other. Subsequent efforts to heal the divisions have meant that many churches have become redundant and are no longer places of worship. The conventional outward signs – crosses, spires, Gothic windows and doors – are still there, but the interiors have been transformed and the buildings have been made into flats or applied to other secular uses.

The revival in the nineteenth century of both the Episcopal Church and the Roman Catholic Church resulted in extensive building programmes, and the churches then erected have usually continued as places of worship. They are to be found all over the North-East, many in small communities. The Roman Catholic Cathedral has the tallest spire in Aberdeen and is mainly the work of a local architect, Alexander Ellis. There are several examples of the work of Sir Ninian Comper in Episcopal churches and notably in St Andrew's Cathedral. Methodists, Baptists, Quakers and Christian Brethren all have places of worship in Aberdeen and elsewhere in the North-East.

The people of the North-East tend not to wear their religious faith on their sleeves. This may be dismissed as lack of zeal, but positively it means that sectarian rivalry and hostility are practically absent. Friendships across the denominations are common, and there are ecumenical sharings of buildings at Bridge of Don and Westhill. These involve the Church of Scotland and the Roman Catholic Church at both, and the Episcopal Church at Westhill. Since 2002, the Kirk of St Nicholas Uniting in Aberdeen has been a Local Ecumenical Partnership comprising congregations of the Church of Scotland and the United Reformed Church.

St Nicholas Kirk houses the unique Jameson embroidered panels. These were intended for a private house and may be an example of seventeenth-century domestic piety, as they portray scenes from the Old Testament and Apocrypha. Some scholars discern in them a hidden commentary on the political divisions of King and Covenant. Less ambiguous is the painted ceiling in the long gallery of Provost Skene's House in Aberdeen. These paintings portray scenes from the life of Christ and also the Arma Christi: the symbols of the Passion. There are carved representations of the Arma Christi at Castle Fraser and Huntly Castle in Aberdeenshire, but the ceiling in Provost Skene's House was long covered in white paint, and the panel at Huntly was badly defaced by a Puritan soldier attacking the castle. Twentieth-century Puritan fervour removed many examples of Victorian piety from the Roman Catholic Cathedral in Aberdeen. This has made room for fine works by recent artists.

Pilgrims with special interests are well provided for in the North-East. There are more sacrament houses here than anywhere else in Scotland, including particularly fine examples in the roofless churches at Auchindoir and Kinkell. There are nine tomb effigies – seven at St Nicholas and two at St Machar's Cathedral. St Machar's has a unique heraldic ceiling dating from the sixteenth century; and there is much fine heraldic decoration in St Andrew's Cathedral. This includes the arms of the American States; and these, and the memorials of Bishop Seabury, make the cathedral a place of pilgrimage for American Episcopalians.

There is a wealth of nineteenth- and twentieth-century stained glass. Douglas Strachan was born in Aberdeen, and he has provided thirty-six windows in the city and thirty in other churches of the North-East. Langstane Kirk in Aberdeen has been deconsecrated but preserves a remarkable collection of windows depicting the life of Christ, by a local artist, John Aiken. Many other Scottish stained-glass artists have enriched the churches of the North-East. King's College Chapel has seven windows by Douglas Strachan and also has the finest medieval carved stalls to be found anywhere in Scotland. These can be contrasted with the twentieth-century wooden furnishings by Tim Stead in St John's Chapel in the Kirk of St Nicholas.

The pilgrim to the North-East should go on by rail or road to the cathedral city of Elgin. Unlike St Machar's, this cathedral did not find a new use as a parish church and is now a magnificent ruin. Pluscarden Abbey, once a ruin, is now being rebuilt. St Brandon's Kirk occupies a site of pre-Christian worship at Birnie and claims to be the oldest church still in use. St Ninian's at Tynet is a church in disguise (it looks like a cottage), and Scalan is a former seminary that looks like a farmhouse. Both recall times when Roman Catholicism was proscribed by law.

The North-East of Scotland may seem to be relatively remote, but there is much to interest and even excite the pilgrim who journeys here.

Henry R. Sefton
*University of Aberdeen*

# Introduction

## Sacred North-East Scotland

The North-East of Scotland is a very distinctive area and constitutes a much larger proportion of the country's land mass than is often realised. It is almost as far from Aberdeen to Inverness as it is from Aberdeen to the Central Belt. Since local-government reorganisation in 1996, the former Kincardineshire has become administratively part of the North-East. Though fully integrated into the Scottish nation for more than 1,000 years, difficulty in communication has allowed the area to develop a very distinctive character, or rather set of characters. The pre-1975 counties took account of variation within the loose framework of being 'the North-East', with Kincardineshire, Aberdeenshire, the City of Aberdeen, Banffshire and Moray (formerly Elginshire) all having rather different characters. Even within these areas there are significant differences, recognised by traditional area names – Gordon, Formartine, Buchan; and superimposed on the whole area is the difference between the coastal towns and villages and the inland agricultural areas.

To anyone from outside the area, the whole of the North-East has something of the fascination of a foreign country. There is the feeling that, under the surface of the people and land of the area, there is something very different from the familiar. This is reflected in language: the so-called Doric is a highly distinctive version of the Scots language; in the building traditions, especially the use of granite; and in the evidence from archaeology of types of

Fig. 1. Birnie Parish Church, Moray

Fig. 2. Monymusk Parish Church,
Aberdeenshire

monument not found elsewhere in Scotland, most notably the recumbent stone circle. This last brings one up firmly against what constitutes the regional sense of sacredness, either of what is worthy of worship or of what symbolises the sense of the 'other', of something beyond and probably above our brief time on this earth. Certainly, the typical stone circles of Aberdeenshire, with the majestic massive recumbent stones which are their distinguishing features, have about them a strong sense of transcendent meaning, recognised at Midmar Church by the juxtaposition of the ancient church site and the much older stone circle. Other evidence of pre-Christian spirituality may be contained in the numerous Class 1 Pictish symbol stones: the post-Christian continuance of the enigmatic symbolism of the earlier stones on stones with crosses suggests some spiritual meaning in those symbols.

As elsewhere in Scotland, Christianity was introduced by both Celtic and Roman missionaries. Distinctive dedications of churches include St Drostan, St Machar, St Ternan, St Palladius, St Rufus and St Laurence. The Normanisation of Scotland in the twelfth century AD covered the North-East, and there are recognisable twelfth-century elements in Birnie church, Moray (Fig. 1); Monymusk, Aberdeenshire (Fig. 2); and in the burgh church of St Nicholas, Aberdeen. The systematic organisation of the Church in Scotland which took place in the twelfth century included the creation of two dioceses to serve the North-East, based in Aberdeen and Elgin (originally at Spynie), though the Diocese of Brechin presumably included at least part of Kincardineshire.

Fig. 3. King's College Chapel, Old Aberdeen,
City of Aberdeen

Fig. 4. Pitsligo Old Parish Church, Rosehearty, Aberdeenshire

Elgin Cathedral, though ruined since the Reformation, is a superb piece of architecture, its quality clear evidence of the fertility of the Laigh of Moray in the later Middle Ages. The surviving fabric of St Machar's Cathedral (**1**) in Old Aberdeen is later, and more distinctively of the North-East, but equally impressive: this was a cathedral of a great trading centre rather than a rich agricultural area. Rivalling St Machar's in scale was the burgh church of Aberdeen, St Nicholas (**13**); but not much medieval fabric remains there. There were only two abbeys in the area, at Deer and Kinloss, and an important priory, Pluscarden (**96**). The remains of Deer and Kinloss are very slight, but the priory church of Pluscarden survived through conversion for Protestant worship to be reclaimed for the Roman Catholic Church in 1943–8. It was restored by the Cistercian monks, whose successors are still there. Another late nineteenth-century restoration was that of the Convent of the Greyfriars in Elgin (**80**).

Of the parish churches from the later Middle Ages there are relatively few survivors, though many later churches probably incorporate medieval fabric. The finest medieval parish church in the North-East is probably at Arbuthnott (**18**), now Aberdeenshire, the oldest part of which dates back to the thirteenth century. So too do parts of Cullen Old (**71**) and Mortlach, both in Moray and still in use. There are several ruined churches which contain significant medieval fabric – though, as they were adapted for Protestant worship after the Reformation, they are not in original condition. They include the old churches of Auchindoir, Deskford, Duffus, Fetteresso, Fordyce, Kincardine O'Neil and Kinkell. A distinctive feature of the churches of Auchindoir, Deskford and Kinkell, and the church of Benholm, is the survival of beautifully decorated sacrament

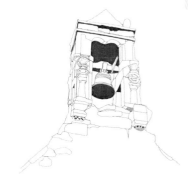

Fig. 5. Belfry, King Edward Old Parish Church, Aberdeenshire

Fig. 6. The former Glenbuchat Parish Church, Aberdeenshire

houses, built into the walls of the church, used to house the Reserved Sacrament after Mass. The respect with which these features were treated after the Reformation says much about the sense of the sacred in the North-East; clearly there was residual affection for the 'Old Religion', as alluded to by Dr Sefton in his Invitation to Pilgrimage above. The finest late Gothic church architecture in the North-East is in Old Aberdeen, at St Machar's Cathedral and King's College Chapel (Fig. 3). The latter, dating from c. 1500, retains much of its original woodwork – a rare pre-Reformation survival.

In the same way as many medieval parish churches were adapted for Reformed use, so too were most of the larger pre-Reformation buildings. At St Machar's Cathedral, the nave was retained and the rest allowed to decay. St Nicholas, Aberdeen was initially divided into two, with separate congregations meeting in the nave (West) and choir (East). At Pluscarden, the choir served as the parish church until

Fig. 7. The former Kinneff Parish Church, now Aberdeenshire

1898. Surviving physical evidence suggests that there was little demand for new church buildings for more than a century after the Reformation in 1560. The shell of one exceptional seventeenth-century building survives at Pitsligo (Fig. 4), near Rosehearty. This was built in 1634, and is on the equal-armed cross plan favoured by the Church of Scotland during its two periods of Episcopal church government in the seventeenth century. The superb laird's pew from the 1634 church was moved

Fig. 8. The former Birse Parish Church, Aberdeenshire

Fig. 9. Bellie Parish Church, Fochabers, Moray

in the late nineteenth century to an adjacent new building, where it can still be seen. There is another fine laird's pew of a little earlier (1602) in Cullen Old Kirk (**71**). Earlier, I alluded to the distinctive building patterns of the North-East. Seventeenth-century evidence of these are the detailing of the larger tower houses, with elaborate corbelling of staircases and bartizans, and more modestly the richly carved belfries of several parish churches in Aberdeenshire. There is a fine one on the 1634 Pitsligo church, and others on the old church of King Edward (c. 1619–20, Fig. 5), at Insch (1613), Tullynessle and Forbes, St Fergus (1644), and more modestly at St Talorgan's, Fordyce (1661). The grandest is at St Congan's Old, Turriff (1635). These belfries are associated with Episcopal church government, and seem to represent a joyous approach to religious observation. A simpler seventeenth-century church is Glenbuchat (Fig. 6), on a T-plan; but comparison with churches in other parts of Scotland suggests that the present form of this building is of the middle decades of the eighteenth century. Roofless seventeenth-century churches include Longside Old (1620), Old Auchterless and St Brandon's, Inverboyndie. A seventeenth-century pulpit survives in St Columba's, Elgin, relocated from an earlier church.

As elsewhere in Scotland, the restoration of Presbyterianism in 1690 was not followed by a spate of new church-building. Indeed, many people in the North-East adhered to Episcopalianism, even though that form of religious observance was proscribed because of its links with Jacobitism. An extreme example

Fig. 10. Dallas Parish Church, Moray

Fig. 11. Peterhead Old Parish Church, Aberdeenshire

of that was the conduct of the congregation of the West Church of St Nicholas, who walked out of that part of the medieval church, which then decayed to such an extent that it had to be completely rebuilt in the 1750s. An interesting early eighteenth-century building which reflects the conservative attitudes of many people in the North-East is Michaelkirk (**74**, 1703), now part of Gordonstoun School, which was designed as a mortuary chapel in late Scots Gothic style, nearly 150 years after that style

had fallen into disrepute. Other churches dating from the first half of the eighteenth century are Speymouth (1733), Spynie (**99**, 1736) and Edinkillie (**77**, 1741), all in Moray; and Kinneff (1738, Fig. 7), now Aberdeenshire. All have since been significantly altered. An important mid-eighteenth-century building (also altered) is St Ninian's Roman Catholic Church (**95**, 1755) at Tynet, Moray – the first Catholic church

Fig. 13. The former Kildrummy Parish Church, Aberdeenshire

built in Scotland since the Reformation. It is claimed that its domestic appearance was intended to distract attention from its function; but it is not at all dissimilar to the typical small Protestant church of the period. At the other end of the scale of size and sophistication is the contemporary West Kirk

Fig. 12. Echt Parish Church, Aberdeenshire

Fig. 14. Bourtie Parish Church, Aberdeenshire

of St Nicholas, Aberdeen, built in the 1750s to architecturally sophisticated designs by James Gibbs.

There is a significant increase in the number of churches surviving in the area from the 1760s and later decades. This is almost certainly a consequence of agricultural improvement, enclosure and road construction. The increased income of the landowners (heritors), and rising population in villages linked to improvement, combined to make new churches both necessary and affordable. In the 1760s, Lumphanan Old, Monquhitter (Cuminestown), Kinloss (**89**) and Tarland Old were built, and a Roman Catholic seminary founded at Scalan (**94**) in upland Banffshire. Churches of this period usually had rectangular windows. Church construction speeded up in the 1770s, with the building of Alves Old, Drumblade, Cruden, Ellon St Mary's (**28**), Garvald, Birse (Fig. 8) and Clatt. Because it was abandoned many years ago, Alves is probably the least altered externally of this group, and, with its round-headed windows, appears to be typical of the period. At Birse and Drumblade, seventeenth-century belfries from earlier buildings were incorporated in the new churches. An important new building of the 1770s is St Mary's, Banff (**22**), comparable in scale to some Lowland burgh churches of the period; its spire was added later. The 1780s and 1790s saw the pace of construction of rural churches increase significantly. Nearly thirty were constructed during this period, too many to itemise. Particularly interesting ones, all in Moray, include Dyke (**78**, 1781), with its original pulpit; St Gregory's, Preshome, a Roman Catholic church in Italian style (**97**, 1788); and Bellie, Fochabers (1798, Fig. 9), a splendid Classical centrepiece for the Duke of Gordon's estate village. More typical churches of the period surviving in use include

Fig. 15. Crimond Parish Church, Aberdeenshire

Fig. 16. Fetteresso Parish Church, Stonehaven, now Aberdeenshire

Rayne (1789) and Tarves (1799), Aberdeenshire, and Dallas (1793, Fig. 10), Moray. Rural depopulation in upland areas has resulted in the abandonment or adaptation of many of the churches of this period. The characteristic rural churches of the later eighteenth and early nineteenth centuries were simple gabled structures with round-arched windows and plain belfries on one gable.

During the French wars of the 1790s and early 1800s, Scottish agriculture benefited from a high level of demand for corn, and thus from high prices. Large classical burgh churches were constructed in Fraserburgh (**32**, 1803), Huntly (1804) and Peterhead (1804–6, Fig. 11), the last-named with advice from an Edinburgh architect. In Aberdeenshire, at Skene (**43**, 1801), Echt (1804, Fig. 12), Kildrummy (1805, Fig. 13) and Bourtie (1806, Fig. 14), refined Georgian Gothic churches were built. The little Roman Catholic church of St Peter, Aberdeen (**14**, 1803) is comparable in style. At the same time, older styles persisted, as at Towie (1803) and Alford St Andrew's (1804). The repertoire of styles acceptable for church design in the North-East increased in the second decade of the nineteenth century. Crimond (1812, Fig. 15) combined a classical steeple with Gothic windows; and the unique Fetteresso, Stonehaven (1810, Fig. 16) introduced castellated turrets and a D-plan to the area. Other churches with Gothic glazing were built at Kennethmont and Chapel of Garioch (**26**) (both 1812).

More correctly Gothic churches were introduced, as elsewhere in Scotland, in this period. The Church of Scotland

Fig. 17. The Annunciation Roman Catholic Church, Portsoy, now Aberdeenshire

favoured the 'Heritors' Gothic' formula of a rectangular plan with a square tower on one end. The earliest example of this in the area appears to be Keith St Rufus (1816–18). It was followed within a few years by Udny (**59**, 1821), Banchory Ternan East (1824), Rafford (1826), Fordoun (1827–9, now Auchenblae Parish Church, **19**) and New Deer (1839–41), and by the Aberdeen churches of St Clement's, Nigg (both 1828) and South (1830).

The Scottish Episcopal and Roman Catholic Churches, building churches on town-centre sites, favoured the 'English College Chapel' style, with gables to the street, crowned with pinnacles. The first of these was what is now St

Fig. 18. Tower, the former North Parish Church, City of Aberdeen

Andrew's Episcopal Cathedral, Aberdeen (**2**, 1816). Later variants on this theme are Holy Trinity Episcopal Church, Elgin (**79**, 1825), Roman Catholic churches at Portsoy (The Annunciation, 1829, Fig. 17) and Tombae (The Incarnation, **100**, 1829), St Andrew's Episcopal Church in Banff (1833), and the Gordon Chapel, Fochabers (**83**, 1834). In modified form, this approach to church design persisted until the late nineteenth century. From this summary, it is evident that, alongside the expansion of the Church of Scotland, both the Scottish Episcopal and Roman Catholic Churches were gaining support in the North-East, and not, as elsewhere in Scotland, by immigration from England and Ireland. This was an indigenous development, and a striking one. For the Roman

Fig. 19. St Giles's Parish Church, Elgin, Moray

Fig. 20. Marnoch Parish Church, Aberchirder, now Aberdeenshire

Catholic Church, the new-found confidence found expression in two new churches built in the 1830s in Italian baroque style, St Thomas's, Keith (**88**, 1831–2) and St Margaret's, Huntly (**35**, 1834). St Thomas's subsequently gained a dome, but St Margaret's is, I would argue, one of the finest church buildings of its period in Scotland. In complete contrast is the former North Church of Scotland, Aberdeen (Fig. 18), solemnly Classical, with a unique spire. Probably the finest church of the period is also classical: St Giles's Church of Scotland, Elgin (1828, Fig. 19), correctly Greek, and replacing a medieval building, a temple to enlightenment and rationality.

Another striking feature of the church history of the North-East is the weakness of the Secession movement in the area. Neither the 1730s secessions (and their subsequent fragmentation) nor the Relief Church had much impact on the area. On the other hand, the grumbling discontent with the influence of the heritors (landowners and town councils) on the appointment of ministers in the established Church of Scotland flared up in the area in a dramatic and profoundly influential way at the end of the 1830s. The 'Intrusion at Marnoch', when the heritors tried to foist an unwanted minister on a Banffshire congregation, was a key event in the run-up to the Disruption in the Church of Scotland in 1843. The Marnoch case also led to the building of a new church (Fig. 20) for the dissenting congregation in the

Fig. 21. Kinneff Parish Church, Roadside of Kinneff, now Aberdeenshire

Fig. 22. King Edward Old Parish Church, Aberdeenshire

village of Aberchirder in 1840. In a similar manner, a church was built in Huntly in 1840–1. Both of these churches joined the Free Church at the Disruption in 1843. The new Church was an immediate success in the area, and many new church buildings were constructed to house the breakaway congregations. The most striking of these was the 'Triple Kirks' in Aberdeen, built rapidly of brick to house three such city-centre congregations. Part of this building survives, but it is much reduced. Other early Free churches in the area are (or were) in Peterhead, Findhorn, Fordyce, Banff, Garmouth, Bucksburn and Roadside of Kinneff (Fig. 21), all built within three or four years after the founding of the new Church. Most were fairly basic structures, but the Banff one, latterly Trinity and Alvah (1844), is a distinguished Classical building. On the outskirts of Aberdeen, the congregation of Woodside took over the recently built parish church, so that a new one had to be constructed in 1846–9. A few new churches were constructed by the continuing Church of Scotland, including King Edward (1848, Fig. 22).

If the Disruption was the most dramatic event in the history of the Church in the 1840s (and arguably in the nineteenth century), the rise and rise of the Scottish Episcopal Church in the North-East is in retrospect equally striking. During the 1840s and 1850s, no fewer than ten new Episcopal churches were built in the area – more than by any other denomination. Particularly notable is St James's, Cruden Bay (**54**, 1842), a very early steepled Gothic Revival building. More modest churches of the period are St Philip's, Catterline (**25**, 1848), All Saints, Woodhead (**62**, 1849, spire 1870), St John the Evangelist,

Fig. 23. Queen's Cross Parish Church, City of Aberdeen

Fig. 24. The former Greyfriars Parish Church,
City of Aberdeen

Longside (**46**, 1853) and All Saints, Whiterashes (**61**, 1858). The Roman Catholic Church also expanded, with new churches at Peterhead (1851), Buckie (**67**, 1857) and Fetternear (1859), and a large new church in Aberdeen, later St Mary's Cathedral (**3**, 1860). Most of these churches were fairly modest, but St Peter's Roman Catholic church in Buckie is notable for its twin spires – a rarity in Scotland. By that time, the Gothic was indisputably the standard style for churches of all denominations; and, for the rest of the nineteenth century, most churches in the North-East were built in variants of Gothic.

The 1840s and 1850s were also noted for the intensity of railway construction, and for industrialisation; and, though the North-East was initially relatively unaffected by these developments, they did have an impact. The period also saw a reduction in grain prices and the beginning of an important transition in Aberdeenshire from agrarian to pastoral farming. The railways allowed specialist beef cattle-rearing to develop, as cattle could now be speedily transported to urban markets. The Aberdeen Angus breed of beef cattle began its rise to prominence during this period. The 1860s saw railway extension, and also a phenomenal growth of church construction; at least thirty new churches were built in the area during that decade. The Free and Scottish Episcopal Churches were the most prolific builders, but a handful of new Church of Scotland buildings were constructed, and the Congregational and United Presbyterian Churches also built new buildings. The United Presbyterians were

Fig. 25. St Mark's Parish Church,
City of Aberdeen

Fig. 26. Queen Street Parish Church,
City of Aberdeen

descendants of the eighteenth-century secessions, but, like their predecessors, were not notably strong in the area. Two of the Episcopal churches were particularly interesting: St Matthew's, Oldmeldrum (**53**, 1863) and St Mary's, Carden Place, Aberdeen (**12**, 1862). The former, with its little steeple, is like a model of a larger church; and at St Mary's the use of different-coloured granites and slates led to its nickname 'the Tartan Kirkie'. Construction of St Mary's led to the bankruptcy of the incumbent.

A feature of the 'true' Gothic Revival, as promoted by A. W. N. Pugin as the only fitting Christian style, was the steeple, soaring towards heaven. The Free Church, perhaps surprisingly, was quick to adopt this feature, for instance at the pioneering Triple Kirks in Aberdeen. Many of the early steeples in the North-East were fairly timid, though the twin steeples of St Peter's Roman Catholic church in Buckie were exceptions, as was the Episcopal church at Forgue. It was in Aberdeen that steeples really flourished, from the late 1860s, with the construction of Gilcomston South (Free, **6**, 1868) and the Langstane Church (Church of Scotland, 1869), facing each other across Union Street. A succession of tall-steepled churches followed, including Ferryhill Free (now Ferryhill, **5**, 1872), Rosemount and Rubislaw (both 1875), Melville Carden Place (United Presbyterian, 1880), Queen's Cross Free (now Queen's Cross, 1881, Fig. 23) and Mannofield (1882). Such was the fashion for steeples that St Mary's Roman Catholic Cathedral acquired one in 1877, and the rebuilding in the 1870s of St Nicholas East after a disastrous fire included the construction of a substantial granite spire. Outside Aberdeen, major steepled churches included Rathen and Braemar Free

Fig. 27. The former Salvation Army
Citadel, City of Aberdeen

Fig. 28. St Peter's Scottish Episcopal Church, Fraserburgh, Aberdeenshire

(now Braemar, **24**, 1869), Tarland (1870, steeple added 1889–90), Ballater (1873–4), Fraserburgh West (1876), Auchterless (1877–9, spire 1896) and Fraserburgh South (**33**, 1879–80). Of these, Rubislaw (1875) is unusual: it was built for the Church of Scotland, then emerging from its post-Disruption decline as a major denomination; it is built of sandstone rather than granite; and it is remarkably ornately detailed. The most striking are, however, Fraserburgh South and Queen's Cross, with their soaring and unorthodox white granite spires. Queen's Cross is one of the finest later nineteenth-century churches in the North-East. In an entirely different approach to the Gothic, Greyfriars, Aberdeen (Fig. 24) was rebuilt in 1891 in an ornate style, its steeple a mass of pinnacles, made possible by the hardness of granite. Just as the North-East was fairly slow to adopt Gothic steeples, so it was slow to relinquish them. The chapel of Blairs College (Roman Catholic, **23**, 1899) has a fine, orthodox one; and the last, St Laurence's, Forres (Church of Scotland, **85**, 1904), has what was probably the last tall Gothic steeple to be built in Scotland.

Classical churches, as in the Central Belt, continued to be built during the currency of the Gothic Revival. After the construction of Trinity and Alvah, Banff, the style lapsed until towards the end of the nineteenth century, when several were built in Aberdeen. The grandest is St Mark's (1892, Fig. 25) with a full-blooded portico and a dome – a notable contrast to the Gothic exuberance of Greyfriars, completed the previous year by the same architect. What is now Queen Street (formerly Free North, 1905, Fig. 26) is less correct, and principally a frontage building, as was John Knox (c. 1900). St Stephen's, Bon Accord Free and Holburn Central are classically detailed but not classical in overall concept. Skene Street Congregational (1886) is a smaller classical building. The Salvation Army Citadel in Castle

Fig. 29. The former St Margaret's Scottish Episcopal Church, Braemar, Aberdeenshire

Street, Aberdeen (1893–6, Fig. 27) is, uniquely, Baronial in style.

An interesting late nineteenth-century development in which the North-East was notably influential was the revival of pre-Reformation worship practice. The Scottish Episcopal Church, increasingly influenced by the Oxford Movement in the Church of England, led the way. The Church of Scotland, anxious to define for itself a distinctive place in the spectrum of Presbyterian denominations, adopted a comparable approach, with Dr Cooper of St Nicholas

Fig. 30. St Thomas's Scottish Episcopal Church, Aboyne, Aberdeenshire

East, Aberdeen, a key figure. New churches built to accommodate this revived approach to worship were not common in the North-East but included Lossiemouth St Gerardine's (**91**, 1901), St Laurence's, Forres (1904) and St Columba's, Elgin (1906). St Gerardine's was designed by the Glasgow architect J. J. Burnet and is one of a family of 'low-line' churches for which he is celebrated. St Columba's is also the work of a Glasgow designer, Peter MacGregor Chalmers, who was the leading practitioner of the turn-of-the-century Romanesque Revival. It is his only church in the North-East. Outstanding Scottish Episcopal churches of the period are St Peter's, Fraserburgh (1891, Fig. 28), with a squat, powerful tower; the Scots Gothic Revival St Margaret's, Braemar (1899–1907, Fig. 29, designed by Sir Ninian Comper to accommodate English summer visitors to upper Deeside); and St Devenick's, Cults (**10**, 1902–3). St Thomas's, Aboyne (**16**, 1909, Fig. 30), also built for summer visitors by a local landowner, was specifically modelled on the owner's English estate church. A fine Roman Catholic church of the time is

Fig. 31. The Sacred Heart Roman Catholic Church, Torry, City of Aberdeen

Fig. 32. High Hilton Parish Church,
City of Aberdeen

the simple but monumental Our Lady of Perpetual Succour, Chapeltown of Glenlivet (**69**, 1899), designed by John Kinross, who also restored the chapel of the Greyfriars Convent of Mercy, Elgin (**80**, 1891–1908).

By the time these churches were constructed, the heroic age of church-building in Scotland had ended. In 1900, the Free Church and the United Presbyterian Church amalgamated as the United Free Church, and, although the new church continued to build, it was not on the scale of its predecessors. The North-East was already well provided with churches on the whole. Cornhill (1904) and Torphins South (1905) were built as United Free churches; and churches at St Cyrus (1904) and Turriff (1909) were probably also constructed for that denomination; and, in Aberdeen, what is now Queen Street Church of Scotland was opened in 1905. The Roman Catholics built an impressive Romanesque Revival church in Torry (1911, Fig. 31), an area prospering as deep-sea fishing from Aberdeen flourished. Church-building virtually ceased during the First World War, though the Scots Gothic Revival Cults West, serving a western suburb of Aberdeen, was completed in 1915–16. Nor were there many churches built in the interwar years. In 1929, the United Free Church and the Church of Scotland united, though some parts of the former stayed out. The first large churches built in the North-East by the enlarged Church of Scotland were in new housing areas in Aberdeen: the High Church, Hilton (1937, Fig. 32), in simplified Romanesque style; and St Mary's, King Street (1938–9, Fig. 33), designed by Aberdeen architect A. G. R. Mackenzie in a style best described as Gothic stripped to essentials. The west front is clearly influenced by that of the nearby St Machar's Cathedral.

The Second World War again halted church-building; but, in the aftermath of that war, Aberdeen, in common with other

Fig. 33. St Mary's Parish Church,
City of Aberdeen

Fig. 34. Summerhill Parish Church,
City of Aberdeen

major centres of population in Scotland, embarked on the construction of large new schemes of local-authority housing to replace old, insanitary city-centre dwellings. From then until the 1970s, scheme followed scheme; and, in the manner of the time, the Church of Scotland through its Church Extension Scheme, and the Roman Catholic Church, provided new places of worship to serve these areas. The first of the Aberdeen schemes was Kincorth, to the south of the city centre, with two churches, Church of Scotland and Our Lady of Aberdeen Roman Catholic church (1963). Mastrick, to the north-west, followed, with Church of Scotland, Roman Catholic (The Holy Family, 1967) and Congregational (1962) churches. There were also extension churches at Garthdee, Summerhill (Fig. 34) and Stockethill. Later Church of Scotland churches were built in Middlefield and Northfield. The last of this series of buildings was St George's, Tillydrone. Most of these buildings are very simple, as cost was an important consideration. The most striking are Summerhill, with its large glazed east end, and the Holy Family, Mastrick, one of a series of polygonal churches designed for the Roman Catholic Church by Charles Grey of Edinburgh.

In the 1970s, the exploitation of North Sea oil brought new prosperity to Aberdeen and a demand for private housing on an unprecedented scale. New churches were built at Bridge of Don (St Columba's, **9**, a church complex shared by the Church of Scotland and Roman Catholic Churches) and in a new suburb west of Aberdeen, Westhill (**60**), where the church is shared by these two denominations and also by the Scottish Episcopal Church. These buildings are of a simple timber-framed type much in favour at the time. Two unusual buildings were, however, also constructed in the later twentieth century. The more unorthodox is the church of the Christian Community, west of

Fig. 35. St Francis of Assisi Roman Catholic
Church, Mannofield, City of Aberdeen

Aberdeen (**15**, 1991). The other, St Francis of Assisi Roman Catholic church, Mannofield (1982, Fig. 35), is only marginally more conventional. The most recent new church building in Aberdeen is Oldmachar, constructed in the early twenty-first century for a 'New Charge' of the Church of Scotland. Other 'New Charges' in the North-East, at Cove and Stockethill, do not have buildings – and Stockethill makes a positive virtue of that. Outside the Aberdeen area, there are, as far as I am aware, no significant post-Second World War church buildings.

As with other booklets in this series, it has been necessary to be highly selective both in describing and in illustrating the church buildings of the North-East. I hope, however, that enough has been written to convince both local people and visitors that the heritage of church buildings in the area is a rich and varied one. Dr Sefton in his Invitation to Pilgrimage has made the point that the people of the North-East have had distinctive attitudes to organised religion for many centuries; and I have tried to reinforce that distinctiveness in highlighting particular buildings and building types in this Introduction. There is, however, no substitute for going out and seeing these buildings in the landscapes and townscapes of an area of great beauty and fascination. Go and see, and engage at first hand with sacred North-East Scotland: it will stay with you for the rest of your lives.

PROFESSOR JOHN R. HUME
*Universities of Glasgow and St Andrews*

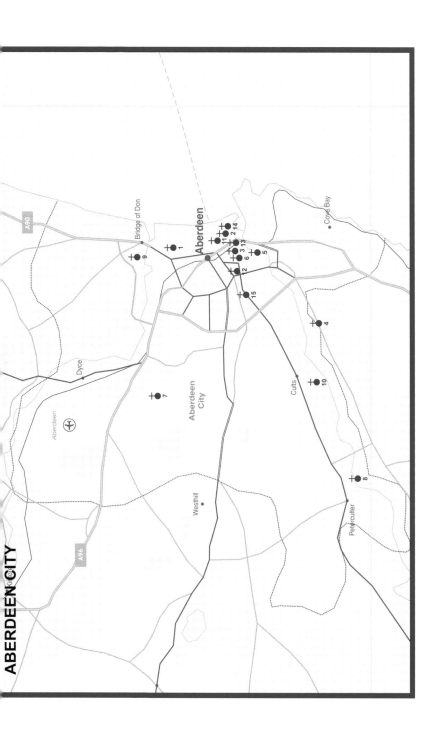

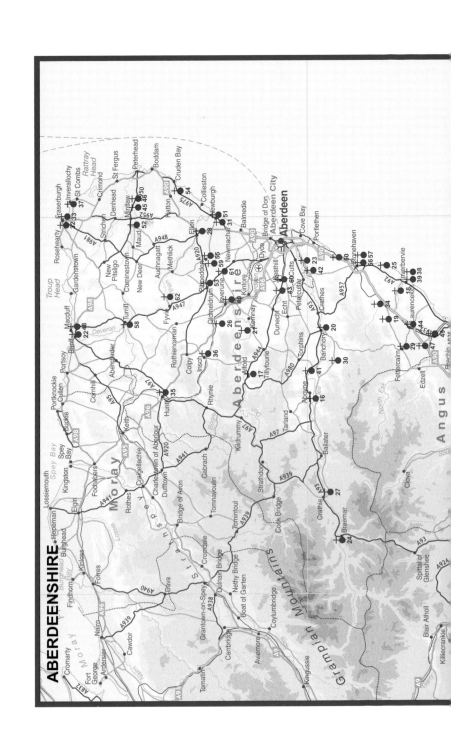

# ABERDEENSHIRE

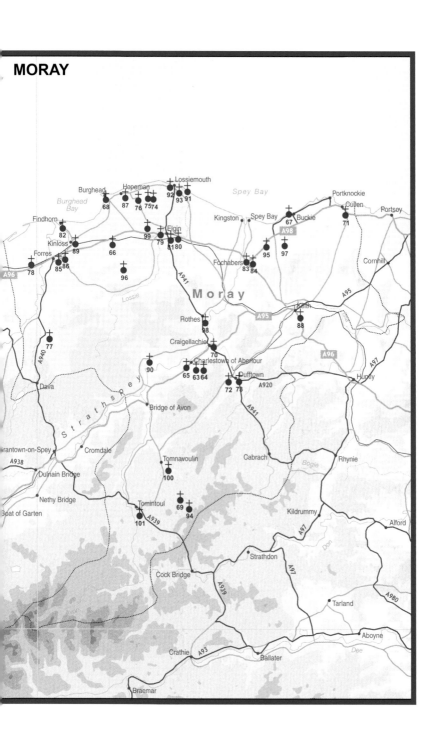

# MORAY

# How to use this Guide

Entries are arranged by local-authority area, with large areas sub-divided for convenience. The number preceding each entry refers to the map. Each entry is followed by symbols for access and facilities:

| | | | |
|---|---|---|---|
| ⅄ | Ordnance Survey reference | 𝄞 | Hearing induction loop for the deaf |
| 🏠 | Denomination | | |
| ⊕ | Church website | 👤 | Welcomers and guides on duty |
| ● | Regular services | 📖 | Guidebooks and souvenirs available/for sale |
| ○ | Church events | | |
| ● | Opening arrangements | NADFAS | Church Recorders' Inventory (NADFAS) |
| ♿ | Wheelchair access for partially abled | ☕ | Refreshments |
| WC | Toilets available for visitors | Ⓐ | Category A listing |
| WC | Toilets adapted for the disabled available for visitors | Ⓑ | Category B listing |
| | | Ⓒ | Category C listing |

**Category A**: Buildings of national or international importance, either architectural or historic, or fine little-altered examples of some particular period, style or building type.

**Category B**: Buildings of regional or more than local importance, or major examples of some particular period, style or building type which may have been altered.

**Category C**: Buildings of local importance, lesser examples of any period, style, or building type, as originally constructed or moderately altered; and simple traditional buildings which group well with others in categories A and B.

*The information appearing in the gazetteer of this guide is supplied by the participating churches. While this is believed to be correct at the time of going to press, Scotland's Churches Scheme cannot accept any responsibility for its accuracy.*

ABERDEEN

## ① CATHEDRAL CHURCH OF ST MACHAR

**The Chanonry
Aberdeen
AB24 1RQ**

🗡 NJ 939 088

🏛 Church of Scotland

🌐 www.stmachar.com

The ancient cathedral of Aberdeen, now consisting of a largely 15th-century nave, although a church has been on the site since about AD 600. Externally, the dominating feature is the 15th-century west front with flanking fortified towers; the towers were added in 1520. The heraldic ceiling of the nave (1520) represents the king and nobility of Scotland, the crowned heads of Europe and the pope and senior clergy in Scotland. Stained glass of mid-19th to mid-20th centuries, including work by Daniel Cottier, Douglas Strachan and William Wilson. Other features include a Celtic cross from about AD 600, baptismal banner in batik by Thetis Blacker, font by Hew Lorimer and notable monuments including plaque to Dr Robert Laws. Triptych in memory of John Barbour, author of 'The Brus'. Willis organ installed 1892 and a peal of eight bells. The church is surrounded by an interesting graveyard.

- Sunday: 11.00am and 6.00pm
- Open April to October 9.00am–5.00pm, November to March 10.00am–4.00pm (01224 485988)

 (in summer)

## ② ST ANDREW'S CATHEDRAL

**King Street
Aberdeen
AB24 5AX**

Ａ NJ 945 065

Ａ Scottish Episcopal

⊕ www.cathedral.aberdeen.
anglican.org

Designed by Archibald Simpson 1817, altered and enhanced by Sir Ninian Comper 1939–45. Gold burnished baldacchino over the high altar. National Memorial to Samuel Seabury, first Bishop of America, consecrated in Aberdeen in 1784. Interesting roof heraldry depicting American states and Jacobite supporters of the 1745 rebellion. Stained glass. Sir John Betjeman described it as one of Aberdeen's best modern buildings. Organ by Bruce of Edinburgh 1818, rebuilt and enlarged by Hill, Norman & Beard.

- Sunday: Holy Communion 8.00am; Sung Eucharist 10.45am; Choral Evensong 6.30pm (July and August, Evening Prayers (Said) 6.30pm); Tuesday: Holy Communion 8.30am; Wednesday: Holy Communion 10.00am and Choral Evensong 6.00pm; Friday: Sung Compline 6.00pm
- Open June to September, Tuesday to Saturday 11.00am–4.00pm or by arrangement (01224 636653)

**ABERDEEN**

**3** ## CATHEDRAL OF ST MARY OF THE ASSUMPTION

**Huntly Street**
**Aberdeen**
**AB10 1SH**

NJ 937 061

Roman Catholic

www.stmaryscathedralaberdeen.org

Off Union Street

The principal church of the Roman Catholic Diocese of Aberdeen, built in 1860 and designed by Alexander Ellis. The tall spire with bells, designed by Robert G. Wilson, was added when the church was elevated to a cathedral. Contains religious artefacts by Charles Blakeman, Gabriel Loire, Ann Davidson, Felix McCullough, David Gulland and Alexander Brodie. The organ is a rare example of the work of James Conacher, Huddersfield, 1887.

- Saturday: Vigil 7.00pm; Sunday: 8.00am, 11.15am, 6.00pm
- Open daily, summer 8.00am–5.00pm, winter 8.00am–4.00pm (01224 640160)

 **4** ## BANCHORY-DEVENICK PARISH CHURCH

**Banchory-Devenick and Maryculter-Cookney Parish Church**

**Banchory-Devenick**
**AB12 5XQ**

NJ 907 024

Church of Scotland

www.bdmc-parish.org.uk

Linked with Maryculter Parish Church (42)

On B9077 Lower Deeside Road, 3km (2 miles) west of the Bridge of Dee

As far as is known, the original kirk was built in the 12th century on the legendary site of St Devenick's tomb. St Devenick was an evangelist, sent out to minister to the Picts and who died in Caithness. The church was rebuilt in 1822 and is the kirk building that stands on this site today, with alterations in 1865 and 1925. A simple rectangular stone-built church with Gothic windows and a neat bellcote.

- 10.30am on 2nd and 4th Sunday of the month
- Open Monday to Friday, 9.00am–12.00 noon (01224 735983)

## 5 FERRYHILL PARISH CHURCH

**Fonthill Road
Aberdeen
AB11 6UD**

Λ  NJ 937 051

🏛  Church of Scotland

🌐  www.ferryhillparishchurch.org.uk

Junction of Fonthill Road and
Polmuir Road

Designed by Duncan McMillan for the Free Church, 1874. Early Gothic-style with a tall square bell-tower with octagonal spire. Side galleries added in 1896 were reduced in 1994. Contains several fine windows by James McLundie, A. L. Moore and others, including a number removed from the former Ferryhill North Church. The sanctuary was reordered 1994, and with new porch and foyer 2000, by Oliver Humphries. The Memorial Chapel incorporates the 51st (Highland) Divisional Signals war memorial, the Piper Alpha and Steele memorial windows, both by Jane Bayliss, and Book of Remembrance. Allen organ. Small museum in the basement.

- Sunday: 11.00am (10.00am in July and August); see notice-boards for evening and weekday services
- Open Monday to Friday, 9.30–11.30am; Saturday 9.30am–12.00 noon. Other times by arrangement (01224 213093)

### 6 GILCOMSTON SOUTH CHURCH

**Union Street
Aberdeen
AB10 1TP**

🏹 NJ 935 059

🏛 Church of Scotland

🌐 www.gilcomston.org

100 metres from west end of Union Street

Striking sandstone and granite building by William Smith, 1868. The slender spire was added in 1875 and rebuilt in 1995. Interior refurbished 2004, LDN Architects. Stained glass by David Gauld, Douglas Strachan and Jane Bayliss. Oak screen and choir stalls. Binns pipe organ, 1902.

- Sunday: 11.00am and 6.30pm; Tuesday: 12.45pm
- Open by arrangement (01224 647144)

### 7 NEWHILLS CHURCH

**Bucksburn
Aberdeen
AB21 9SS**

🏹 NJ 876 095

🏛 Church of Scotland

🌐 http://newhillschurch.org.uk

The present church was built in 1830 to a design by Archibald Simpson, near to the site of the original 17th-century church (now part of the graveyard). Painted coat of arms of the patron, Lord James Hay of Seaton, and the Earl of Fife, and several modern banners, add colour to the interior.

- Sunday: 10.30am and 6.00pm (not July and August)
- Open Monday to Friday, 9.00am–1.00pm (01224 716161)

 (by arrangement)

## 8 PETERCULTER PARISH CHURCH

**North Deeside Road
Peterculter
Aberdeen
AB15 9ET**

 NJ 841 007

Church of Scotland

www.culterkirk.co.uk

Prominently sited on the main road, this church was built in 1895 as the Free Church. Gothic-style in grey granite with a square tower and a rose window above the entrance. An extension built in 1995 provides a meeting place; extensive refurbishment in 2001 has created a multi-purpose sanctuary used by the local community.

- Sunday: 10.30am; Thursday: 11.30am
- Open by arrangement (01224 735845)

## 9 ST COLUMBA'S PARISH CHURCH

**Braehead Way
Bridge of Don
Aberdeen
AB22 8RR**

NJ 935 104

Church of Scotland/
Roman Catholic

www.stcolumbaschurch.org.uk

St Columba's Parish Church was built in 1983 in partnership with the local Roman Catholic congregation. Two pyramid-roofed pavilions provide the church and hall with other accommodation in the link between. The most notable feature is a steel cross at the rear of the church.

- Church of Scotland: Sunday 10.00am and 6.00pm; Roman Catholic: Sunday 9.45am, Wednesday, Friday and Saturday 10.00am
- Open by arrangement (01224 825653)

## 10 ST DEVENICK'S, BIELDSIDE

**North Deeside Road
Bieldside
Aberdeen
AB15 9AP**

⚔ NJ 882 025

⛪ Scottish Episcopal

🌐 www.stdevenicks.org.uk

Pink-and-grey granite church, designed by Arthur Clyne and opened in 1903. Organ (Wadsworth) installed in 1910: 'best specimen of its kind by Wadsworth ever placed in Aberdeen or for a considerable distance round about'. North transept completed in 1959 by building of Lady Chapel, which seats 24. West gallery and foyer added in 2000.

- Sunday: 8.30am, 10.30am; Thursday: 10.30am
- Open by arrangement (01224 863574)

## 11 ST MARGARET OF SCOTLAND

**Gallowgate
Aberdeen
AB25 1EA**

⚔ NJ 942 067

⛪ Scottish Episcopal

🌐 www.stmargaretsgallowgate.
org.uk

Just north of Marischal College

Dedicated in 1869, the spacious sanctuary includes many fine examples of the work of Sir Ninian Comper, including the Chapel of St Nicholas, the first building he designed and with the original stained glass and the Chapel of the Holy Name, a gift in memory of his parents. His style is mainly Early English with elements of Byzantine and Renaissance. Memorial garden.

- Sunday: Mass 10.30am, Evensong 7.00pm
- Open Tuesday morning 10.00am–12.00 noon. Other times by arrangement (01224 872960 or 01224 644969)

## 12 ST MARY'S CHURCH, CARDEN PLACE

**Carden Place
Aberdeen
AB10 1UN**

A NJ 929 060

🏛 Scottish Episcopal

🌐 http://stmarysepiscopal.co.uk

Between Skene Street and Queen's Road

The variety of granites and patterned roof tiles earned it the nickname 'the Tartan Kirkie'. To a design by Alexander Ellis and Rev. F. G. Lee, dating from 1864. The east end sustained severe damage during an air raid in April 1943. Reconstructed 1952. Altar triptych by Westlake (c. 1862) in the crypt. The church is home to a Samuel Green chamber organ, built in 1778. Display of historical photographs in the choir vestry (1905) adjoining the church.

- Sunday: 8.00am and 10.15am; Tuesday: 7.00pm; Wednesday: 10.00am
- Open Friday 11.00am–2.00pm for prayer and reflection, or by arrangement (01224 584123)

## 13 KIRK OF ST NICHOLAS UNITING

**Back Wynd
Aberdeen
AB10 1JZ**

A NJ 941 063

🏛 Church of Scotland /
United Reformed Church

🌐 www.kirk-of-st-nicholas.org.uk

The 'Mither Kirk' of Aberdeen dates from the 12th century. The present building is largely 18th- and 19th-century. The west end 1755 by James Gibbs, the east end by Archibald Simpson 1837. The church contains the Chapel of the Oil Industry, and the 15th-century St Mary's Chapel. West Kirk: 3-manual organ by Willis 1881/1927; East Kirk: organ by Compton 1933; St John's Chapel: organ by Brewsher & Fleetwood 1825. The carillon of 48 bells is the largest in Great Britain. Seventeenth-century embroidered wall hangings.

- Sunday: 11.00am; Daily Prayers, Monday to Friday: 1.05pm
- Open May to September, Monday to Friday 12.00 noon–4.00pm. Other times by arrangement (01224 643494)

**14** ST PETER'S CHURCH

**3 Chapel Court**
**Justice Street**
**Aberdeen**
**AB11 5HX**

⚔ NJ 946 064

⛪ Roman Catholic

🌐 www.stpetersaberdeen.org.uk

Off the Castlegate

Aberdeen's hidden gem, this is the oldest Catholic church in Aberdeen. Designed by James Massie, 1803–4; gallery added 1815 and façade finished 1817 by Harry Leith. Within the courtyard is the residence occupied since 1774, including by, in the 18th century, the Vicars Apostolic of the Lowland district, Bishop James Grant and Bishop John Geddes.

• Saturday: Vigil 6.00pm; Sunday: 11.00am; weekdays as announced
• Open Tuesday, Thursday and Friday 11.00am–4.30pm, or by arrangement (01224 626359)

**15** THE CHRISTIAN COMMUNITY

**8 Spademill Road**
**Aberdeen**
**AB15 4XW**

⚔ NJ 919 056

⛪ Christian Community

🌐 www.thechristiancommunity. co.uk

Situated in the west end of Aberdeen, this small church was built in 1991, by Camphill Architects, to house community facilities as well as priest's office and vestry. Simple interior in lilac wash lit by four flanking windows; the altar is lit only by candles. Oak candle-holders, altar and pulpit. Altar painting by David Newbatt, a local artist.

• Sunday: 9.30am children's service; 10.30am Act of Consecration of Man (Communion)
• Open by arrangement (01224 208109)

# 16 ST THOMAS'S, ABOYNE

**Ballater Road
Aboyne
AB34 5JL**

NO 521 986

Scottish Episcopal

At junction of A93 with B9094

Consecrated 1909, gifted by George Coats, 1st Baron Glentanar and designed by Fryers & Penman of Largs. This stone-built church with a square tower topped with a stone spire was modelled on the Early English Burrough Church in Leicestershire. East window by Morris & Co.; 16th- and 17th-century Flemish and Spanish stained-glass medallions in other windows. Organ by Abbott & Smith, 2009. Centenary project to develop grounds to comply with 'Eco-congregation in Scotland' guidelines.

- Sunday: 11.15am – 1st Sunday, family service; 2nd, Holy Communion; 3rd and 5th, family communion; 4th, Matins
- Open by arrangement (01339 755726)

# 17 HOWE TRINITY PARISH CHURCH, ALFORD

**110 Main Street
Alford
AB33 8AD**

NJ 582 157

Church of Scotland

www.howetrinity.org.uk

Designed by James Souttar and built in 1867 as Alford Free Church, and substantially reordered in 2001 by William Lippe Architects to mark the union of Alford, Keig and Tullynessle & Forbes. Renovations include reorientation of chancel to the long wall; pews replaced with chairs; creation of glass vestibule. Set of engravings showing the Parable of the Sower in modern form and stained-glass window of the Burning Bush by Jane Bayliss. New halls with sweeping curved roof, 2008, William Lippe Architects.

- Sunday: 10.00am
- Open by arrangement (01975 562282)

ABERDEENSHIRE

**ABERDEENSHIRE**

### 18 ST TERNAN'S CHURCH, ARBUTHNOTT

**Arbuthnott
AB30 1NA**

🏹 NO 801 746

⛪ Church of Scotland

🌐 www.arbuthnottbervieand
kinneff.org.uk

Linked with Bervie (38)

On the B967, 4.5km (3 miles) from Inverbervie

Almost certainly a St Ternan cult church long before it became a parish church by the late 12th century. The chancel dates from the early 13th century, the Arbuthnott family aisle and the bell-tower from the late 15th century. The nave is medieval or earlier. The church was gutted by fire in 1889 and reopened in 1890; architect A. Marshall Mackenzie. 1-manual and pedal organ by Wadsworth 1890, a 'small but resourceful instrument'. The unique Arbuthnott Missal, Psalter and Prayer Book (now in Paisley Museum) were transcribed and illuminated in the Priest's Room above the Arbuthnott Aisle between 1497 and 1500.

- Sunday: 10.00am
- Open daily (01561 362584)

  (July and August)

### 19 AUCHENBLAE PARISH CHURCH

**St Palladius, West Mearns Parish**

**Auchenblae
AB30 1WQ**

🏹 NO 726 784

⛪ Church of Scotland

Linked with Fettercairn Parish Church (29), Glenbervie Parish Church (34)

Near Laurencekirk

Designed by John Smith in 1829 as Fordoun Parish Church on a site known as Kirkton of Fordoun. Religious site since the 7th century. St Palladius died and was reputedly buried here. Celtic stone in vestibule. Memorial to first Protestant martyr George Wishart in graveyard. Stained-glass rose window.

- Sunday: 11.00am, excluding 1st Sunday of the month
- Open by arrangement (01561 340203)

## 20 ST TERNAN'S EPISCOPAL, BANCHORY

**High Street
Banchory
AB31 5TB**

A NO 694 957

Scottish Episcopal

Opposite Town Hall

St Ternan's was founded in 1851 with help from the local landowners, and it has adapted to changes such as the arrival of the railway in 1853 and two world wars. Designed by William Ramage, the unassuming oblong exterior with belfry belies the nicely detailed interior. The hall, by Jim Hammond 1985, won a Kincardine & Deeside Design Award.

- Sunday: 8.00am and 11.00am (children's activities in term-time); Tuesday: 9.00am; Thursday: 10.15am
- Open every day during daylight hours (01330 822783)

## 21 BLAIRDAFF PARISH CHURCH

**Cairnley
Blairdaff
AB51 5LS**

A NJ 704 173

Church of Scotland

www.blairdaffandchapelof gariochchurch.org.uk/index.html

1.5km (1 mile) south-east of Blairdaff on the road to Kemnay

Blairdaff Church was originally built in 1850 as the Free Church and became the parish church in 1934. Blairdaff and Chapel of Garioch Parish Church were united in 2007 creating one congregation with two centres of worship. Built in the local granite, it is a typical Church of Scotland building without a spire or tower. Inside is a U-plan gallery and the original pulpit with sounding board.

- Sunday: 9.30am
- Open by arrangement (01467 681543 or 01464 851466)

**ABERDEENSHIRE**

## 22 BANFF PARISH CHURCH

**High Street
Banff
AB45 1AE**

NJ 689 638
Church of Scotland
www.banffparishchurchof
scotland.co.uk

Built in 1789–90, Andrew Wilson architect and builder, with tower and spire added 1828–9 to design by William Robertson, Elgin; completed by Thomas Mackenzie, Elgin, 1849. Chancel added and interior altered 1929. Stained glass. Small chapel created at rear of church 1994. Pulpit, font, communion table and stained glass in chancel all gifted 1929. Other furnishings from Trinity & Alvah Church, united 1994.

- Sunday: 11.00am (church) and (except July and August) 6.30pm (hall)
- Open 2.00–4.00pm July and August or by arrangement (01261 812107)

## 23 ST MARY'S CHAPEL, BLAIRS

**Blairs
AB12 5YQ**

NJ 883 009
Roman Catholic
www.blairsmuseum.com

On B9077, South Deeside Road, 6.5km (4 miles) south of Aberdeen

Former collegiate chapel, designed by Richard Curran of Warrington, opened in 1901. The walls originally had painted decoration, but in 1911 were lined with marble. At the same time were added the reredos and baldacchino in carved wood with figures of the Scottish patron saints, Andrew and Margaret. Fine stained-glass windows. The Blairs Museum is adjacent to the chapel.

- Sunday: 9.00am
- Open Monday, Tuesday and Thursday 10.30am–2.00pm; Saturday and Sunday by arrangement (01224 780351)

## 24 BRAEMAR CHURCH

**Clunie Bank Road
Braemar
AB35 5YY**

A NO 150 913

Church of Scotland

www.braemarandcrathieparish.
org.uk

Linked with Crathie Kirk (27)

Behind the Braemar Mews

The inspiration for the building of this former Free Church in 1870 was Rev. Hugh Cobban. Unusually, he was buried in the church, behind the pulpit. Gothic, cruciform church with tower and spire. In the apse are four lancet stained-glass windows with lilies, a branch with fruit and a tree with palms. Some interesting tapestry banners, described as 'living pictures'.

- Sunday: 10.00am
- Open 9.00am–9.00pm, April to October (01339 742208)

## 25 ST PHILIP'S, CATTERLINE

**Catterline
AB39 2UL**

A NO 869 789

Scottish Episcopal

www.nmearnssec.org.uk

Linked with St Ternan's, Muchalls (50), St James the Great, Stonehaven (56)

Off A92 between Montrose and Stonehaven

St Ninian was reputed to have landed at Catterline. The present building, designed in Early English style by Charles Brand, dates from 1848 and was built on the site of an earlier church, retaining its historic graveyard. Simple church of nave and chancel with a small porch. The interior has been recently refurbished. Near Dunnottar Castle.

- Sunday: 10.15am
- Open daily (01569 764264)

**ABERDEENSHIRE**

##  CHAPEL OF GARIOCH

### Chapel of Garioch
**AB51 5HE**

🚶 NJ 716 242

⛪ Church of Scotland

🌐 www.blairdaffandchapelof
gariochchurch.org.uk/index.html

In centre of village

The present church, dating from 1813, was built on the site of a 12th-century church. Subsequent changes include a chancel built out from the north wall and the impressive stained-glass window. Of particular interest are the baptismal basin of 1742, the mosaic plaque and the A-listed gateway in the west wall of the churchyard, dated 1626.

• See notice-board, or telephone for information about services
• Open by arrangement (01467 681543 or 01464 851466)

 (Church)  (Gateway)

## 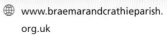 CRATHIE KIRK

### Crathie
**AB35 5UN**

🚶 NO 265 949

⛪ Church of Scotland

🌐 www.braemarandcrathieparish.
org.uk

Linked with Braemar Church (24)

On A93 Ballater–Braemar road

Queen Victoria laid the foundation stone in 1893; the church opened 1895. Neat Gothic cruciform church with square tower and short spire designed by A. Marshall Mackenzie. The granite church stands on a hill overlooking the ruins of the 14th-century church and the River Dee. Memorial stones, plaques and stained glass commemorate royalty and ministers. Fine Iona marble communion table and 17th-century oak reredos.

• Sunday: 11.30am
• Open April to October, Monday to Saturday 9.30am–5.00pm; Sunday 12.45–5.00pm (01339 742208)

## 28 ST MARY ON THE ROCK, ELLON

### South Road
### Ellon
### AB41 9NP

 NJ 958 301

Scottish Episcopal

🌐 www.stmarystjames.org.uk

Linked with St James's Church, Cruden Bay (54)

On A90/A948 at south end of the town

A superb example of the work of George Edmund Street, built in 1871 to incorporate chancel, nave, narthex and spire. Floor tiles by Minton. Good glass, including windows by Clayton & Bell on the north side of the nave, Lavers & Barreau on the south side, all dating from the 1880s, and by Jane Bayliss 1996.

- Sunday: 8.30am and 11.00am; Wednesday: 10.00am in St Mary's Hall
- Open daily 10.00am to dusk (01358 720366)

## 29 FETTERCAIRN PARISH CHURCH

### West Mearns Parish

### Fettercairn
### AB30 1UE

 NO 651 735

Church of Scotland

Linked with Auchenblae Parish Church (19), Glenbervie Parish Church (34)

On B9120 to Laurencekirk

Constructed of red sandstone, Fettercairn Parish Church is set high on a mound surrounded by an ancient graveyard. Built in 1803 and with the steeple added in 1860, the building was completely refurbished and extended in 1926. The interior has interesting stained glass and locally made furnishings.

- Sunday: 9.30am
- Open by arrangement (01561 340203)

**BIRSE AND FEUGHSIDE PARISH CHURCH**

**Finzean Church**

**Finzean
AB31 6NY**

A NO 617 924

Church of Scotland

www.birseandfeughside.org.uk

Between Banchory and Aboyne on South Deeside Road

This mission church was erected by Francis Farquharson, Laird of Finzean, in 1863. It was refurbished in 2005 with meeting rooms, kitchen, toilet and storage facilities being added, and now has modern audiovisual equipment which is used to enhance morning worship. Several large banners are displayed. An eco-garden is being created to the north of the church.

- Sunday: 11.00am
- Open by arrangement (01330 850329)

**31 FOVERAN PARISH CHURCH**

**Foveran
AB41 6AB**

A NJ 985 241

Church of Scotland

http://foveran-parish-church.org

Linked with Holyrood Chapel, Newburgh (51)

1.5km (1 mile) south of Newburgh on A975

Built 1794, organ apse added 1900, interior refurbished 1934 with pews and fittings from the demolished Foveran United Free Church. Early 15th-century Turing Stone, 17th-century bust of Sir John Turing, Queen Anne hour-glass attached to pulpit and font using carved medieval column. Various monuments including bronze plaque to painter and etcher James McBey, born nearby.

- Sunday: 11.00am (shared with Holyrood Chapel, Newburgh)
- Open by arrangement (01358 789288)

## 32 FRASERBURGH OLD PARISH CHURCH

**The Square
Fraserburgh
AB43 9HH**

 NJ 998 671

Church of Scotland

www.fraserburgholdparish
church.org.uk

The present building dates from 1801, with a church on this site since 1572. Classical Georgian church designed by Alexander Morrice. The pulpit is one of the tallest in Scotland, and the superb memorial window designed by Douglas Strachan, 1906, was gifted by Sir George Anderson, Treasurer of the Bank of Scotland, in memory of his parents. A front pew in the south gallery is marked as the place where Marconi, pioneer of wireless telegraphy, worshipped during his stay in Fraserburgh. Forster & Andrews 2-manual organ of 1892.

- Sunday: 11.00am and 6.00pm
- Open daily July and August (01346 510139 or 01346 515332)

     (in Church Centre)

## 33 FRASERBURGH SOUTH PARISH CHURCH

**19 Seaforth Street
Fraserburgh
AB43 9BD**

 NJ 999 667

Church of Scotland

www.southkirk.com

Linked with Inverallochy and Rathen East Church (37)

Erected 1878, architect John B. Pirie, in a blend of white-and-pink granite characteristic of his work. Variously described as French or German Gothic. Fine interior of Art Nouveau design: gallery, pulpit, iron-framed gallery front and timber-lined walls in natural honey colour. Square tower with lancet windows topped with a round stone spire flanked by pinnacles.

- Sunday: 9.30am May to September, 10.15am October to April
- Open June to August, Tuesday to Friday 10.00am–4.00pm or by arrangement (01346 518244)

**34 GLENBERVIE PARISH CHURCH**

**West Mearns Parish**

**Glenbervie
AB39 3XW**

 NO 766 807

Church of Scotland

Linked with Auchenblae Parish Church (19), Fettercairn Parish Church (29)

Near Stonehaven

Gothic hall-church of 1826 preserving original design and features. The exterior is given character by pinnacles at the corners and gables. Oil lamps electrified. Stones preserved and sheltered. Grandparents of Robert Burns buried in old kirkyard.

- Sunday: 11.00am, 1st Sunday of the month
- Open by arrangement (01561 340203)

 **35 ST MARGARET'S CHURCH, HUNTLY**

**Chapel Street
Huntly
AB54 8BS**

NJ 528 402

Roman Catholic

Linked with St Thomas's, Keith (88)

Octagonal church with impressive classical front façade built 1834. The architect was William Robertson of Elgin in collaboration with Bishop James Kyle. Spire 24m (8oft) with fine toned bell. Altar piece and other paintings from the Gordon family of Xeres, Spain, 1840. Restored 1990 by Doric Construction, Aberdeen. Organ by Peter Conacher, 1871.

- Sunday: 9.45am
- Open most days until 4.00pm or by arrangement (01466 792435)

##  36 ST DROSTAN, INSCH

**Commerce Street
Insch
AB51 0BT**

NJ 630 281

Scottish Episcopal

Linked with St Matthew and St George, Oldmeldrum (53), All Saints', Whiterashes (61), All Saints', Woodhead of Fetterletter (62)

On B992 off A96

Alexander Ross, 1894. Agreeable rustic Gothic in red granite with sandstone dressings. Red-tiled roof with broach-spired wooden bellcote. Font 1892, and screen 1904. Twelfth-century grave marker or coffin slab to Radulfus, Chaplain to the Bishop of Aberdeen.

- Sung Eucharist 10.00am 2nd and 4th Sunday of the month
- Open by arrangement (01651 872208)

## 37 INVERALLOCHY AND RATHEN EAST CHURCH

**Rathen Road
Inverallochy
AB43 8YB**

NK 041 650

Church of Scotland

www.inverallochykirk.com

Linked with Fraserburgh South Parish Church (33)

B9033, 4.5km (3 miles) south-east of Fraserburgh

Gothic church of 1842 with subsequent alterations and extensions. T-plan with later octagonal spirelet. Squared rubble with pinnings typical of the area. Fixed pews in the gallery and moveable seating in the nave.

- Sunday: 11.00am May to September, 11.30am October to April
- Open by arrangement (01346 518244)

## 38 BERVIE PARISH CHURCH, INVERBERVIE

**43 King Street
Inverbervie
DD10 0RQ**

⌖ NO 830 727

⛪ Church of Scotland

🌐 www.arbuthnottbervieand
kinneff.org.uk/

Linked with St Ternan's Church, Arbuthnott (18)

In centre of town

Built in 1836 by architect John Smith, with elegant clock and bell-tower. Two stained-glass windows originally from United Free Church. Lawton pipe organ, 1904. To mark the millennium, new doors were fitted between the inner vestibule and sanctuary. Doors with stained-glass overlay panels depicting significant local landmarks and buildings, including the church.

• Sunday: 11.30am
• Open by arrangement (01561 362584)

## 39 KING DAVID OF SCOTLAND CHURCH, INVERBERVIE

**St David's Episcopal Church**

**Victoria Terrace
Inverbervie
DD10 0PS**

⌖ NO 828 733

⛪ Scottish Episcopal /
Roman Catholic

Small, simple church with very pretty interior. Shared with the local Roman Catholic community.

• Episcopal: Holy Communion, Sunday 9.30am; Roman Catholic: Mass, Saturday 6.30pm
• Open daily 9.00am–4.30pm (01356 622708)

**ABERDEENSHIRE**

## 40 INVERURIE WEST PARISH CHURCH

**17 West High Street
Inverurie
AB51 3SA**

NJ 774 216

Church of Scotland

www.inveruriewestchurch.org

Built in 1876 as a Free Church. Designed in a Gothic style by Donald McMillan with nave and corner spire. The Acorn Centre was created in 2008: the church was split in two by adding a new floor at gallery level to give a worship, conference and concert facility upstairs and a hospitality area downstairs, meeting the needs of a whole range of people in the community. The original features of the church are retained, including a stained-glass rose window, while the change is announced by the new glass porch.

- Sunday: 11.00am
- Open daily 10.00am–4.00pm (01467 670850)

(Acorn Centre)

## 41 CHRIST CHURCH, KINCARDINE O'NEIL

**Kincardine O'Neil
AB34 5AA**

NO 590 997

Scottish Episcopal

On A93, North Deeside Road

Small Episcopal church in the middle of Royal Deeside; built in 1866, this was probably the last building designed by William Ramage. Nave and chancel under a roof with a single ridge-line, embellished with pretty cresting and a belfry (restored 2006). Fine collection of mainly Victorian stained-glass windows and charming wrought-iron railings enhance the interior. Organ, c. 1850s, installed in 1998. The church has bucked the recent trend by increasing its congregation.

- Sunday: 10.00am (not 5th Sunday), 6.00pm on 5th Sunday of the month
- Open by arrangement (01339 884225)

## 42 MARYCULTER PARISH CHURCH, KIRKTON OF MARYCULTER

**Banchory-Devenick and Maryculter-Cookney Parish Church**

### Kirkton of Maryculter
### AB12 5FS

⅄ NO 857 992

🏰 Church of Scotland

🌐 www.bdmc-parish.org.uk

Linked with Banchory-Devenick Parish Church (4)

A church was founded in this area by the Knights Templar; the ruin of the original St Mary's church is close to the River Dee. Maryculter Church dates from 1787, extended 1882. Wooden furniture and box pews. Very pretty stained-glass windows feature the four Evangelists and Peter, Paul, James and Jude. The church buildings have been extended to include a fully equipped modern office, kitchen, meeting rooms and toilets. Everyone welcome.

- 10.30am on 1st, 3rd and 5th Sunday
- Open Monday to Friday 9.00am–12.00 noon (01224 725983)

## 43 SKENE PARISH CHURCH, KIRKTON OF SKENE

Kirkton of Skene

### Kirkton of Skene
### AB32 6XX

⅄ NJ 803 077

🏰 Church of Scotland

Linked with Trinity Church, Westhill (60)

Off A944 Aberdeen–Alford road

The church was built in 1801, architects William and Andrew Clerk, as a plain rectangular building with the pulpit in the centre of the south wall. In 1932, the interior was entirely refurnished and the sanctuary moved to the east wall. Stained glass by Blair & Blyth. A mortsafe outside the west door is an interesting historical object.

- Sunday: 11.15am
- Open by arrangement (01224 743277)

 (Wed 2.00–4.00pm)

## 44 LAURENCEKIRK CHURCH

**6 High Street
Laurencekirk
AB30 1AE**

 NO 718 716

 Church of Scotland

Linked with Luthermuir Church
(47), Marykirk (49)

There has been a church on this
site since the 13th century. The present
building is of 1804, enlarged 1819, and
the bell-tower with its short spire
designed by Matthew & Mackenzie
added in 1895. It is a rectangular
building of red sandstone with large
windows with Gothic tracery. There is
a gallery within and several stained-
glass windows.

- Sunday: 11.00am
- Open by arrangement (01561 378838)

## 45 LONGSIDE PARISH CHURCH

**Inn Brae
Longside
AB42 2XG**

 NK 037 473

 Church of Scotland

 http://linux.c-mar.com/~church/
index.html

Impressive rectangular building by
John Smith, 1836. The west gable is
capped by a bellcote. The adjoining
old parish church, a roofless ruin,
dates from 1620 and is accessed
through a lychgate of 1705. Some
notable monuments in the graveyard.

- Sunday: 11.00am
- Open by arrangement (01779 821224)

**ABERDEENSHIRE**

### 46 ST JOHN THE EVANGELIST, LONGSIDE

**Peterhead Road
Longside
AB42 4XX**

 NK 039 473

 Scottish Episcopal

On A950 at east end of village

Built 1853 to a design by William Hay. A large building with many fine features, including saddleback tower, stained glass by Chance and one by J. Hamilton depicting St Margaret of Scotland. Superb reredos of Caen stone with figures and scenes from the Bible. On display are many rare items belonging to Rev. John Skinner of Linshart, Rector for 65 years (1742–1807), also known as Tullochgorum, poet and writer.

- Sunday: 10.00am
- Open May to October, 8.30am–6.00pm, or via contact in entrance porch (01779 472217)

   (in halls)

### 47 LUTHERMUIR CHURCH

**Aberluthnott Parish**

**Church Road
Luthermuir
AB30 1YS**

 NO 655 686

 Church of Scotland

Linked with Laurencekirk Church (44), Marykirk (49)

3km (2 miles) north of A90 (turn off at North Water Bridge)

Originally built as Muirton Secession Church in 1780 with a turf roof. Rebuilt 1822 with a near-square plan, later Gothicised and the wood and wrought-iron bellcote added. The pews were removed in the 1990s and replaced with individual chairs. One stained-glass rose window depicts a descending dove.

- 9.30am on 2nd and 4th Sunday of the month
- Open by arrangement (01561 378838)

### 48 MACDUFF PARISH CHURCH

**Church Street
Macduff
AB44 1UN**

⚔ NJ 701 643

⛪ Church of Scotland

🌐 www.macduffparishchurch.org.uk

Once used to guide boats to safe haven, this white box kirk of 1805 high on the bluff above the harbour was transformed in 1865 by architect James Matthews of Aberdeen into a striking landmark, with notable stained-glass windows and a lovely three-storey tower with a lead-domed roof and cupola above. Galleried interior, most of the fittings dating from 1865. Magnificent views. Nearby stand the town cross and an anchor, symbolic of the message of the church.

• Sunday: 11.00am and 6.00pm
• Open by arrangement (01261 832316)

### 49 MARYKIRK

**Aberluthnott Parish**

**Marykirk
AB30 1UT**

⚔ NO 687 656

⛪ Church of Scotland

Linked with Laurencekirk Church (44), Luthermuir Church (47)

The present building dates from 1806, being a replacement for the church whose ruins are adjacent. The building is a simple rectangle with Gothic windows and a Victorian bellcote (1893, by James Matthews). The galleried interior has been much altered and embellished. Gothic Revival font. The Thornton Aisle sits in the midst of the graveyard, with ancient gravestones.

• 9.30am on 1st and 3rd Sunday of the month
• Open by arrangement (01561 378838)

## 50 ST TERNAN'S, MUCHALLS

**Muchalls
AB39 3PP**

NO 891 921

Scottish Episcopal

www.nmearnssec.org.uk

Linked with St Philip's, Catterline (25), St James the Great, Stonehaven (56)

By Stonehaven

The oldest church building in the Diocese of Brechin, built in 1831 as a simple country church. The chancel, designed by Alexander Ellis, was added in 1870. Attractive furnishings adorn the interior, with a plain chancel arch leading to the chancel and apse.

- Sunday: 10.30am Holy Communion
- Open daily 10.00am–4.00pm (01569 762433)

 (Mon, Wed)

## 51 HOLYROOD CHAPEL, NEWBURGH

**Main Street
Newburgh
AB41 0BE**

NJ 999 253

Church of Scotland

http://foveran-parish-church.org

Linked with Foveran Parish Church (31)

Built in 1838 as the original Newburgh Mathers school; converted as Chapel of Ease for Foveran Parish Church 1882. Clock tower added 1892, interior refurbished 1907, including pitch-pine roof in imitation of St Laurence, Forres. Named in honour of the original medieval Chapel of the Holy Rood and St Thomas the Martyr in Inch Road, Newburgh, all that remains of this is the Udny Family Mausoleum in the Holyrood Cemetery.

- Sunday: 11.00am (shared with Foveran Parish Church)
- Open by arrangement (01358 289236)

## 52 DEER PARISH CHURCH, OLD DEER

### Old Deer
### AB42 5LN

 NJ 979 477

Church of Scotland

Built in 1789 as a simple rectangular church with Venetian windows to the east and west. The front porch with tower and spire were added in the late 1890s to a design by Sir George Reid, PRSA. The pulpit table and font are by A. Marshall Mackenzie, 1898. Willis pipe organ of the 1890s. Stained-glass windows in memory of George Smith, local benefactor who emigrated to America, and Rev. Dr Kemp, minister from 1899 to 1953, and his wife.

- Sunday: 10.30am
- Open by arrangement (01771 623582)

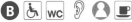

## 53 ST MATTHEW AND ST GEORGE, OLDMELDRUM

### Urquhart Road
### Oldmeldrum
### AB51 0AD

NJ 812 279

Scottish Episcopal

Linked with St Drostan, Insch (36), All Saints', Whiterashes (61), All Saints', Woodhead of Fetterletter (62)

North end of village on A947

Ross & Joass, 1863. Pleasing granite Early Decorated with striking chequered voussoirs to west window. Octagonal spire alongside the simple nave and chancel. Tendril-like freestone tracery is carved with real freedom. Stained glass by Hardman records the Life of Our Lord. Intricate Arts and Crafts monument to Beauchamp Colclough Urquhart of Meldrum.

- Sunday: Sung Eucharist 11.30am
- Open by arrangement (01651 872208)

**ABERDEENSHIRE**

 **54** ## ST JAMES'S CHURCH, CRUDEN BAY, PETERHEAD

**Chapel Hill
Cruden Bay
Peterhead
AB42 0SF**

A  NK 069 356

Scottish Episcopal

www.stmarystjames.org.uk

Linked with St Mary on the Rock, Ellon (28)

2.5km (1.5 miles) west of Cruden Bay on A975

The tall, pinnacled tower and spire of St James's can be seen from miles around. Designed by William Hay in 1842, the church has a nave and chancel with the tower and spire at the west end. The font is from the chantry chapel, built after the battle between the Scots and the Danes in 1012.

- Sunday: 9.30am Eucharist
- Open daily 10.00am to dusk (01358 720366)

 **55** ## PITMEDDEN CHURCH

**Pitmedden
AB41 7NX**

A  NJ 893 274

Church of Scotland

www.uppc.org.uk

Linked with Udny Parish Church (59)

Near Udny

Disruption church built in 1864. Gothic rectangle in pink granite with buttresses separating the windows in the side walls. Three-lancet window above pointed arched entrance. Clock- and bell-tower with square spire to the side. Egyptian-style interior.

- Sunday: 10.00am
- Open by arrangement (01651 842052)

The Cathedral Church of St Machar   1

St Andrew's Cathedral   2

Cathedral of St Mary of the Assumption   3

St Ternan's Church, Arbuthnott   18

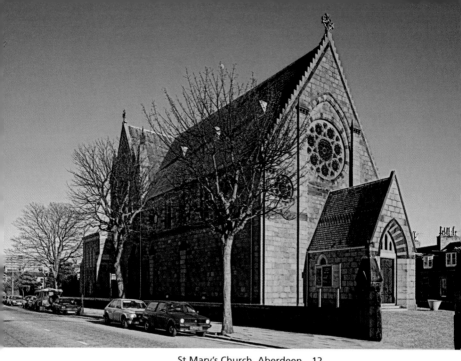

St Mary's Church, Aberdeen 12

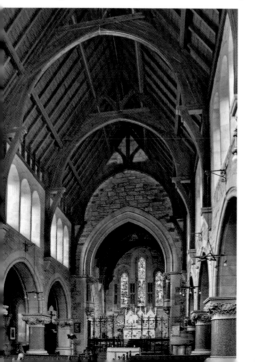

Old Kirk of Cullen   71

St Philip's, Catterline   25

Macduff Parish Church   48                    Gordon Chapel, Fochabers   83

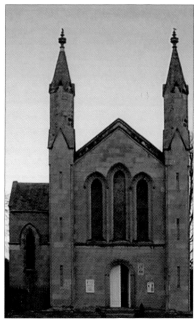

St Ninian's Church, Tynet   95

Knockando Parish Church   90

St James the Great, Stonehaven   56

Dyke Parish Church   78

Spynie Parish Church   99

Old Seminary, Scalan   94

St Margaret of Scotland, Aberlour    64

St Margaret of Scotland, Lossiemouth    92

**56** ### ST JAMES THE GREAT, STONEHAVEN

**Arbuthnott Street
Stonehaven
AB39 2JB**

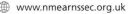

NO 873 857

Scottish Episcopal

www.nmearnssec.org.uk

Linked with St Philip's, Catterline (25), St Ternan's, Muchalls (50)

Off south side of Market Square

The nave was designed by Sir Robert Rowand Anderson in 1877 in Norman/Early English style. The chancel was added in 1885 and the narthex and baptistry in 1906 by Arthur Clyne. Baptistry glass by Sir Ninian Comper 1929. Elaborately sculptured reredos by Gambier-Parry of London. 2-manual organ of some merit by Wadsworth 1881/5.

- Sunday: 8.30am and 10.30am; Wednesday: 10.30am
- Open daily (01569 764264)

 **57** ### CHURCH OF THE IMMACULATE CONCEPTION (ST MARY'S), STONEHAVEN

**Arbuthnott Place
Bridgefield
Stonehaven
AB39 2FY**

NO 875 856

Roman Catholic

Small Gothic church of 1877 by J. Russell Mackenzie which is an architectural gem. The elaborately detailed façade and four-stage tower with spire have details derived from Poitiers and Chartres. Church and presbytery were founded by Elsa Mona Richart Hepburn in memory of her daughter and husband. Stations of the Cross were painted in 1954 by F. Walterson, a Shetland artist.

- Sunday: 9.00am and 11.00am. Saturday: 6.30pm at St David's Episcopal Church, Inverbervie
- Open daily 8.00am–6.00pm (01569 762433)

**58** ST CONGAN'S, TURRIFF

**Deveron Road
Turriff
AB53 7BB**

A NJ 722 498

Scottish Episcopal

Elegant church by William Ramage, 1862, with a red, slender Gothic western tower. Mural tablet of Bishop Jolly, who is depicted in the east window. Beautiful stained glass. Oak rood screen, pulpit and lectern are the important ornaments. A short distance away are the ruins of the medieval church, whose elaborate bellcote of 1635 survives.

- Sunday: 11.30am (winter), 10.30am (Easter to end October); Wednesday: 10.00am
- Open by arrangement (01888 562530)

**59** UDNY PARISH CHURCH

**Udny Green
AB41 7RS**

A NJ 880 264

Church of Scotland

www.uppc.org.uk

Linked with Pitmedden Church (55)

This handsome late-Georgian square church of 1821 by John Smith with crenallated and pinnacled tower stands at the top of one of Scotland's few village greens. The interior was remodelled by A. Marshall Mackenzie in 1891. Very fine stained-glass window. Harrison & Harrison manual-action pipe organ. The circular stone morthouse of 1823 kept coffins securely under lock and key for up to three months.

- Sunday: 11.15am
- Open by arrangement (01651 842052)

 B

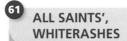

## 60 TRINITY CHURCH, WESTHILL

**Westhill Drive**
**Westhill**
**AB32 6FY**

NJ 833 072

Church of Scotland/Scottish Episcopal/Roman Catholic

Linked with Skene Parish Church (43)

Off A944 Aberdeen–Alford road

Ecumenical and multi-purpose building of 1981 designed by Stock Brothers with extension completed in 2003. Used by the Church of Scotland, the Scottish Episcopal Church and the Roman Catholic Church.

- Sunday: Roman Catholic 9.00am; Church of Scotland 10.00am; Scottish Episcopal 11.15am
- Open most of the week (01224 743277)

## 61 ALL SAINTS', WHITERASHES

**Whiterashes**
**AB21 0QP**

NJ 855 235

Scottish Episcopal

Linked with St Drostan, Insch (36), St Matthew and St George, Oldmeldrum (53), All Saints', Woodhead of Fetterletter (62)

On A947, 4.5km (3 miles) south of Oldmeldrum

Gothic-style nave and chancel church designed by James Matthews in 1858. In use as a school until 1885, after which it was dedicated to St Drostan. Windows by Sir Ninian Comper, 1890, featuring saints chosen for the Christian names of the Irvines of Drum and Straloch.

- Evensong 3.00pm, 1st Sunday of the month
- Open by arrangement (01651 872208)

ABERDEENSHIRE

**62** ALL SAINTS',
WOODHEAD OF
FETTERLETTER

**Woodhead
AB53 9PL**

A NJ 790 385

🚪 Scottish Episcopal

Linked with St Drostan, Insch
(36), St Matthew and St George,
Oldmeldrum (53), All Saints',
Whiterashes (61)

1.5km (1 mile) east of Fyvie

Early English aisleless nave and
chancel by John Henderson 1849. The
fine tower with the slated broach
spire was added in 1870. Described
by Rev. John B. Pratt in *Buchan* (1870)
as one of the finest examples of a
Scottish village church. Crosses and a
sheaf of arrows from Fyvie Priory are
incorporated in the walls. The altar
and reredos are from St Margaret's,
Forgue. Organ by David Hamilton
of Edinburgh, recently restored by
Sandy Edmonstone.

- Sunday: 10.15am
- Open by arrangement (01651 872208)

**63** ABERLOUR PARISH
CHURCH

**The Square
Aberlour
AB38 9QB**

A NJ 266 430

🚪 Church of Scotland

🌐 www.speyside.moray.org/
Aberlour/thekirk.htm

Linked with Craigellachie Parish
Church (70)

Originally dedicated to St Drostan,
the church was built in 1812. The
neo-Norman tower, 1840, by William
Robertson, architect, Elgin, was the
sole survivor of a disastrous fire
in 1861. George Petrie, architect,
rebuilt the church in neo-Norman
style. Choir added 1933 to a design
by J. Wittet in memory of Sir James
Ritchie Findlay. First organ by
Brindley & Foster 1900, rebuilt by
Ernest Lawton 1932, and present
organ rebuilt by Sandy Edmonstone
1991.

- Sunday: 11.00am
- Open by arrangement (01340 871027)

**64**

## ST MARGARET OF SCOTLAND, ABERLOUR

**High Street
Aberlour
AB38 9QD**

⋀ NJ 272 431

♨ Scottish Episcopal

⊕ www.trinityelgin.org

Linked with St Michael's, Dufftown (72), Holy Trinity, Elgin (79), St Margaret of Scotland, Lossiemouth (92)

Designed by Alexander Ross and consecrated in 1879, the tall Gothic church retains its splendid original interior. Built for the local Episcopal congregation and the orphanage 120 years ago; the feet of hundreds of children have worn down the Victorian tiled floor. Lovely carvings of flowers, birds and squirrels on pillar capitals and screen arch. Organ originally built by Harrison, 1879.

- Sunday: 11.00am, 1st Sunday of the month; 9.15am other Sundays
- Key from Aberlour Hotel (01340 871287)

**65**

## CHURCH OF THE SACRED HEART, ABERLOUR

**Chapel Terrace
Aberlour
AB38 9LL**

⋀ NJ 266 426

♨ Roman Catholic

⊕ http://stsylvesters.net

Linked with Our Lady of Perpetual Succour, Chapeltown (69), St Mary's, Dufftown (73), St Sylvester's, Elgin (81), St Columba's, Lossiemouth (93), Church of the Incarnation, Tombae (100), St Michael's, Tomintoul (101)

A small, simple and unpretentious church, overlooking the Speyside towns of Aberlour and Craigellachie. Designed by Archibald McPherson, architect, Edinburgh, it was opened in 1909. It is built of stone with a slate roof and Gothic touches in the windows. The interior is surprisingly rich with a carved and gilded wooden screen and canopied reredos.

- Saturday: 5.00pm
- Open by arrangement (01343 542280)

## 66 ALVES CHURCH

**Alves
IV30 8UR**

🏛 NJ 125 616
⛪ Church of Scotland
🌐 www.abcofs.org.uk

Linked with Burghead Church
(68), Findhorn Church (82), Kinloss
Church (89)

Just south of A96, 1.5km (1 mile) west
of Alves village

Built in 1845 to a design by Thomas
Mackenzie of Elgin but only
completed in 1878 by architects
A. & W. Reid & Melvin, Elgin. United
with the North Church in 1931. An
imposing symmetrical building
with round-headed windows and a
square tower capped by a balustrade
and urns. Alves Parish Church was
originally a prebend held by the
Chantor of Elgin Cathedral.

- Sunday: 11.30am, 1st Sunday of the
  month
- Open by arrangement (01309 690931)

## 67 ST PETER'S CHURCH, BUCKIE

**St Andrew's Square
Buckie
AB56 1QN**

🏛 NJ 419 653
⛪ Roman Catholic

Linked with St Mary's, Fochabers,
(84), St Ninian's Church, Tynet (95),
St Gregory's Church, Preshome (97)

To plans donated by Bishop Kyle and
supervised by A. & W. Reid of Elgin.
Dedicated on a site donated by Sir
William Gordon. Rose window. High
altar of Italian marble surrounded
by murals depicting *The Calming of
the Storm* and *The Walking on the Water*.
Reredos and baptistry, C. J. Menart
1907. Statue of Our Lady of Aberdeen,
copy of original in Brussels. Organ
originally by Bryceson 1875, recently
installed here from Fort Augustus
Abbey.

- Saturday: Vigil Mass 6.30pm; Sunday:
  10.00am; weekdays: 9.30am, except
  Thursday and Saturday
- Open by arrangement (01542 832196)

Ⓐ ♿ wc 👂 📖

##  BURGHEAD CHURCH

**Grant Street
Burghead
IV36 2RB**

A NJ 114 688

Church of Scotland

www.abcofs.org.uk

Linked with Alves Church (66), Findhorn Church (82), Kinloss Church (89)

Built as the United Free Church by Mr Anderson of Hopeman in 1861, extended and gallery added 1908. The parish church began as a chapel of ease of Duffus Kirk in 1823 and a successor church opened in 1902. After the Union of 1929, the United Free Church was used. Stained glass by Father Giles Connacher of Pluscarden Abbey using *dalles de verre* technique. Bell from original chapel of ease.

- Sunday: 11.30am
- Open by arrangement (01309 690931)

##  OUR LADY OF PERPETUAL SUCCOUR, CHAPELTOWN

**Chapeltown
Braes of Glenlivet
AB37 9JS**

A NJ 242 210

Roman Catholic

http://stsylvesters.net

Linked with Aberlour (65), Dufftown (73), Elgin (81), Lossiemouth (93), Tombae (100), Tomintoul (101)

4.5km (3 miles) east of B9008, turn off at Auchnarrow

Pink granite Scottish Romanesque church with tower. Built 1896–7 in farmland setting encircled by hills, designed by John Kinross, replacing an earlier building of 1828. Vivid stencil decoration illuminates the interior. Finely carved chancel rails, pulpit, altar and reredos.

- 9.30am every 3rd Sunday in rotation with Tombae and Tomintoul
- Open by arrangement (01807 580226)

**70** **CRAIGELLACHIE PARISH CHURCH**

**Victoria Street
Craigellachie
Aberlour
AB38 9QB**

NJ 290 452

Church of Scotland

www.speyside.moray.org/
Aberlour/thekirk.htm

**Linked with Aberlour Parish Church (63)**

In centre of Craigellachie on A96 to Keith

Built on a site overlooking the River Spey as a mission church from Aberlour. Simple T-plan church with Gothic details, built in the local pink granite with a slate roof. Inside, a traditional layout with the pulpit in the centre of the long wall. A meeting room constructed in 2002 provides a useful resource.

- Sunday: 9.45am
- Open by arrangement (01340 871027)

**71** **OLD KIRK OF CULLEN**

**Old Cullen
AB56 4XW**

NJ 507 664

Church of Scotland

1km (½ mile) south-west of Cullen town centre

This 13th-century church was originally dedicated to St Mary the Virgin and is the burial place of the 'interior parts' of Queen Elizabeth de Burgh (died 1327). A chaplainry was endowed here by Robert I in 1327, and the church acquired collegiate status in 1543. Later additions include the St Anne's Aisle of 1539, while there is a fine example of a laird's loft 1602. Other features include a pre-Reformation aumbry or sacrament house, tombs and monuments including one to James, 1st Earl of Seafield, Chancellor of Scotland at the Treaty of Union of 1707, and 17th-century box pews. The churchyard has many interesting and imposing tombs, monuments and gravestones.

- Sunday: 10.30am
- Open summer 2.00–4.00pm Tuesday and Friday, or by arrangement (01542 841453)

## 72 ST MICHAEL'S, DUFFTOWN

**Conval Street
Dufftown
AB55 4AH**

NJ 322 398

Scottish Episcopal

www.trinityelgin.org

Linked with St Margaret of Scotland, Aberlour (64), Holy Trinity, Elgin (79), St Margaret of Scotland, Lossiemouth (92)

Charming small Gothic Revival church by Alexander Ross, 1881.

- Sunday: 11.00am Eucharist and, on 1st Sunday of the month, 9.30am Eucharist, 11.00am Matins
- Open daily 10.00am–5.00pm (01343 547505)

## 73 ST MARY'S, DUFFTOWN

**Fife Street
Dufftown
AB55 4AP**

NJ 327 399

Roman Catholic

http://stsylvesters.net

Linked with Sacred Heart, Aberlour (65), Our Lady of Perpetual Succour, Chapeltown (69), St Sylvester's, Elgin (81), St Columba's, Lossiemouth (93), Church of the Incarnation, Tombae (100), St Michael's, Tomintoul (101)

Built near to the ancient foundation of Mortlach Kirk, St Mary's is currently lined up for extensive restoration. Designed by William Robertson in 1824-6, it is a classical church with Gothic trimmings; the façade is ornamented with buttresses and a pierced balustrade. Inside, Gothic touches are given by the Stations of the Cross and the ribbed plaster vault. A large painting of the Assumption of the Virgin Mary hangs over the high altar.

- Thursday: 10.00am
- Open by arrangement (01343 542280)

**MORAY**

## 74 THE MICHAEL KIRK, GORDONSTOUN

**Gordonstoun School
Duffus
IV30 5QZ**

NJ 193 689

Interdenominational

www.gordonstoun.org.uk

1.5km (1 mile) east of Duffus, 8km (5 miles) north of Elgin

Reached by footpath from Gordonstoun (the 'silent' walk), this dignified little church was built in 1705 as a mausoleum for 'the Wizard Laird', Sir Robert Gordon, on the site of the ancient Kirk of Ogstoun. Roofed, furnished and fitted by John Kinross in 1900 for Lady Gordon-Cumming. Remarkable window tracery enhanced by flower carvings.

- Holy Communion 8.40am most Sundays during the academic year; candlelit Compline 9.00pm, Thursdays during winter term
- Open by arrangement (01343 837837)

## 75 ST CHRISTOPHER'S, GORDONSTOUN

**Gordonstoun School
Duffus
IV30 5QZ**

NJ 184 690

Interdenominational

www.gordonstoun.org.uk

1.5km (1 mile) east of Duffus, 8km (5 miles) north of Elgin

Gordonstoun School was founded in 1934 by Kurt Hahn with the aim of encouraging self-reliance and independence. St Christopher's is the main school chapel, built 1965–6 to designs by former pupil Patrick Huggins, to complement the Michael Kirk. Seating is 'gathered about the lectern pulpit and the Communion Table', whose positions emphasise the equal importance of Word and Sacrament while giving space for orchestral or dramatic performances.

- Main school service: Sunday 10.45am during term-time
- Open by arrangement (01343 837837)

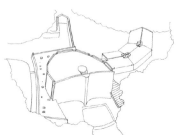

##  76 DUFFUS PARISH CHURCH

**Hopeman Road**
**Duffus**
**IV30 5RR**

NJ 168 687

Church of Scotland

www.duffusparish.co.uk

Linked with Hopeman Parish Church (87), Spynie Parish Church (99)

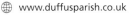

The present kirk of 1869 is by A. & W. Reid in Gothic Revival style with tower and spire. It replaced the old kirk of St Peter's (situated half a mile eastwards on the Gordonstoun Road), whose walls still stand. As early as the 13th century, a church stood on the old site.

• See website for details
• Open by arrangement (01343 830276)

##  77 EDINKILLIE PARISH CHURCH, DUNPHAIL

**Edinkillie**
**Dunphail**
**IV36 0QH**

NJ 020 466

Church of Scotland

Linked with Dyke Parish Church (78)

14.5km (9 miles) south of Forres

Small church built 1741 in traditional 18th-century style. Central pulpit and galleries on three sides. Fine pipe organ. Watch-house in the well-kept graveyard. Beautifully situated on the banks of the River Divie.

• Sunday: 12.00 noon
• Open by arrangement (01309 611271)

**MORAY**

## 78 DYKE PARISH CHURCH

**Dyke
IV36 2TL**

NH 990 584

Church of Scotland

Linked with Edinkillie Parish Church (77)

Off A96, 4.5km (3 miles) west of Forres

Noble Georgian rectangular church built 1781. The Rodney Stone, a 9th-century Pictish symbol stone, was found in the churchyard during the digging of the foundations; it was set up on a site in Brodie Castle grounds to commemorate the victory of Admiral Lord Rodney over the French and Spanish fleets at Dominica in 1782. Interesting crypt and triple pulpit (one of only two in Scotland). Close to Brodie Castle.

- Sunday: 10.00am
- Open by arrangement (01309 641257)

## 79 HOLY TRINITY, ELGIN

**Trinity Place
Elgin
IV30 1UL**

NJ 214 630

Scottish Episcopal

www.trinityelgin.org

Linked with St Margaret of Scotland, Aberlour (64), St Michael's, Dufftown (72), St Margaret of Scotland, Lossiemouth (92)

Gothic style on a Greek-cross ground plan to a design by William Robertson of Elgin, 1826. The crenellated and pinnacled south entrance gable, intended as an architectural feature visible from the High Street, is now blocked by the ring road. Chancel added 1852 and interior recast; nave lengthened 1879. Plain dignified interior with late 19th-century stained glass.

- Sunday: Holy Communion 8.00am, Family Eucharist 11.00am, Evensong 6.30pm; Monday: Holy Communion 5.45pm; Tuesday: 9.00am; Wednesday: 8.00am; Friday: 11.00am
- Open daily 9.00am–5.30pm (01343 547505)

## 80 GREYFRIARS CONVENT OF MERCY, ELGIN

**15–19 Abbey Street**
**Elgin**
**IV30 1DA**

NJ 219 628

Roman Catholic

Beautiful and careful restoration (1891–1908) by architect John Kinross, for the 3rd Marquess of Bute, of a 15th-century Franciscan friary. Magnificently carved oak screen divides the choir from the nave, and a splendid barrel-vaulted ceiling stretches unbroken to the stained-glass window above the altar. Fine cloister with original medieval well.

- Masses: Tuesday 10.00am and Friday 7.00pm
- Open by arrangement (01343 547806)

## 81 ST SYLVESTER'S, ELGIN

**Institution Road**
**Elgin**
**IV30 1QT**

NJ 219 626

Roman Catholic

http://stsylvesters.net

Linked with Aberlour (65), Chapeltown (69), Dufftown (73), Lossiemouth (93), Tombae (100), Tomintoul (101)

The church and presbytery were designed and completed in 1844, architect Thomas Mackenzie of Elgin. Dedication in recognition of the financial support by the younger brother of Sir William Drummond of Grantully, who took the name Sylvester on converting to Catholicism. Lady Chapel altar 1915, by R. B. Pratt. Sanctuary altered 1968 in keeping with the new liturgy. Major alterations to church and adjoining school 2000 to form sacristy and meeting rooms, by Ashley Bartlam Partnership. Large cross by the monks of Pluscarden.

- Saturday: Vigil 7.00pm; Sunday: 11.45am
- Open by arrangement (01343 542280)

MORAY

## 82 FINDHORN CHURCH

**Findhorn
IV36 3YL**

⚲ NJ 042 642

⛪ Church of Scotland

🌐 www.kinlossandfindhorn
church.org.uk

Linked with Alves Church (66),
Burghead Church (68), Kinloss
Church (89)

On main street of Findhorn village

This is the third Findhorn village, the
site of the previous two now lying
under the sea. Findhorn consists of
rows of fishermen's cottages, gable-
end to the water in the local manner.
The church was built as Kinloss Free
Church in 1843 to a design by John
Urquhart of Forres. A handsome
building in stone with a pretty tower
and lunette windows high in the
north and south walls.

- Sunday: 10.00am, alternating with
  Kinloss
- Open by arrangement (01309 690153
  (am) or 01309 691288 (pm))

## 83 GORDON CHAPEL, FOCHABERS

**Castle Street
Fochabers
IV32 7DW**

⚲ NJ 346 589

⛪ Scottish Episcopal

🌐 www.gordonchapel.org.uk

Built 1834 to a design by Archibald
Simpson, restored 1874. The church is
upstairs with the rectory (originally
a school) below. The exceptionally
fine Burne-Jones windows, made
by William Morris & Co., were added
between 1874 and 1919. Each of the
windows commemorates a member
or members of the Gordon Lennox
family. Fine organ by Hill 1874. CCTV
of services in downstairs room, which
has disabled access.

- Sunday: 10.00am Eucharist with
  hymns; see church notice-board for
  other services
- Open daily 10.00am–4.00pm (01542
  882782)

## 84 ST MARY'S, FOCHABERS

**South Street
Fochabers
IV32 7ED**

NJ 347 586

Roman Catholic

Linked with St Peter's Church, Buckie (67), St Ninian's Church, Tynet (95), St Gregory's Church, Preshome (97)

The foundation stone for this Gothic chapel was laid in 1825, architect J. Gillespie Graham. Pretty stone façade with pinnacled buttresses, traceried windows and delicate parapet above the central door. Chancel added 1905. Beautifully sculpted cream stone altar.

• Sunday: 12.00 noon; weekdays: 10.00am
• Open daily (01542 832196)

## 85 ST LAURENCE PARISH CHURCH, FORRES

**High Street
Forres
IV36 1BU**

NJ 035 588

Church of Scotland

Built on a site of Christian worship dating from the mid-13th century, today's neo-Gothic building – designed by John Robertson and dedicated in 1906 – is a fine example of the stonemason's craft. The stained-glass windows by Douglas Strachan and Percy Bacon help to create the special atmosphere of peace and beauty. Font is a replica of one in Dryburgh Abbey.

• Sunday: 10.00am
• Open May to September, Monday to Friday 10.00am–12.00 noon, 2.00–4.00pm. Other times by arrangement (01309 672260)

**MORAY**

 **86 ST JOHN'S CHURCH, FORRES**

**Victoria Road
Forres
IV30 3BN**

⚐ NJ 041 592

⛪ Scottish Episcopal

🌐 http://myweb.tiscali.co.uk/stjohns forres/

Built 1830–40 by Patrick Wilson, architect; remodelled and enlarged in Italianate style by Thomas Mackenzie, 1844. The building has been beautified over the years, including the laying of mosaic tiles throughout the chancel and aisles. The frontage is adorned with a wheel window, the entrance sheltered by an arcaded logia and flanked by a campanile. A large canvas in the apse, 1906, and mural behind the font, 1911, are the work of William Hole, RSA.

- Sunday: 8.00am, 10.00am
- Open daylight hours, or key at Rectory (01309 672856)

 **87 HOPEMAN PARISH CHURCH**

**Farquhar Street
Hopeman
IV30 5SL**

⚐ NJ 145 693

⛪ Church of Scotland

🌐 www.duffusparish.co.uk

Linked with Duffus Parish Church (76), Spynie Parish Church (99)

Cruciform church of 1854 with Tudor Gothic clock tower added 1923. Opened for worship as a Free Church, in 1901 it became Hopeman United Free Church, and in 1929 the UF Church united with the old Church of Scotland.

- Sunday: 10.00am except 1st Sunday of the month, when there is a service at 10.30am at Duffus or Spynie – see website for further details
- Open by arrangement (01343 830276)

## 88 ST THOMAS'S, KEITH

**Chapel Street
Keith
AB55 5AL**

NJ 430 502

Roman Catholic

Linked with St Margaret's Church, Huntly (35)

Designed 1831, architect William Robertson of Elgin. Successor to 1785 chapel and cottage at Kempcairn, following planning and fund-raising by Father Lovi. Roman Doric pilastered exterior and 'plain' interior with nave and sanctuary. Enlarged with copper-clad dome, altar, communion rails, pulpit and oak pews 1915. Altarpiece painting *The Incredulity of St Thomas*, commissioned by Charles X of France 1828. Fine stained-glass windows 1970s. St John Ogilvie Chapel commemorating saint born nearby. Extensive restoration 1996.

- Saturday: Vigil 6:30pm; Sunday: 9:30am
- Open daily, dawn to dusk (01542 882352)

## 89 KINLOSS CHURCH

**Kinloss
IV36 3GH**

NJ 063 617

Church of Scotland

www.kinlossandfindhorn
church.org.uk

Linked with Alves Church (66), Burghead Church (68), Findhorn Church (82)

At west end of Kinloss, on B9011

The present church, built 1765, is an elegant rectangle. The crenellated tower was added and the interior remodelled by A. & W. Reid of Elgin, 1863. Before the mid-17th century, the congregation met in the chapterhouse of Kinloss Abbey (founded 1151), of which only ruins remain. Money raised from the sale of stones from the Abbey was used to build the first parish church, in use before 1657.

- Sunday: 10.00am, alternating with Findhorn
- Open by arrangement (01309 691105 or 01309 690349)

**MORAY**

**90 KNOCKANDO PARISH CHURCH**

**Knockando
AB38 7RY**

NJ 186 429

Church of Scotland

Turn off B9102 at Cardhu

Award-winning design for new church by Law & Dunbar-Nasmith Partnership, 1993, on the site of an earlier building destroyed by fire in 1990. The design, including a Celtic-inspired round tower, is sympathetic with the previous building. The Creation is symbolised in a new stained-glass window by Andrew Lawson-Johnson. Watch-house in the kirkyard.

- Sunday: 10.30am
- Open Wednesday only, 2.00–4.00pm July and August (01340 831381)

**91 ST GERARDINE'S HIGH, LOSSIEMOUTH**

**St Gerardine's Road
Lossiemouth
IV31 6JY**

NJ 233 706

Church of Scotland

Foundation stone laid 1898; building of Norman design by Sir John J. Burnet. The plainness of the Norman tower, white harled walls and red roof belie the magnificent interior. The features include many items of stained glass depicting various Biblical themes. The history of the parish, recently researched, goes back to AD 710.

- Sunday: 11.00am and 6.00pm
- Open by arrangement (01343 813146)

## 92 ST MARGARET OF SCOTLAND, LOSSIEMOUTH

**Stotfield Road
Lossiemouth
IV31 6QS**

🅰 NJ 227 706

⛪ Scottish Episcopal

🌐 www.trinityelgin.org

Linked with St Margaret of Scotland, Aberlour (64), St Michael's, Dufftown (72), Holy Trinity, Elgin (79)

Small church of 1922 with Gothic detailing built to a design by Alexander Ross of Inverness, responsible for Episcopal churches great and small throughout the north, including Inverness Cathedral. Simple interior with open timber-vaulted ceiling.

- Sunday: Parish Eucharist 9.30am; Thursday: Eucharist 10.00am and Eventide Prayer 5.30pm
- Open by arrangement (01343 547505)

## 93 ST COLUMBA'S, LOSSIEMOUTH

**Union Street
Lossiemouth
IV31 6BG**

🅰 NJ 232 709

⛪ Roman Catholic

🌐 http://stsylvesters.net

Linked with Sacred Heart, Aberlour (65), Our Lady of Perpetual Succour, Chapeltown (69), St Mary's, Dufftown (73), St Sylvester's, Elgin (81), Church of the Incarnation, Tombae (100), St Michael's, Tomintoul (101)

Small church in the shape of a Latin cross, designed by Arthur Harrison of Stockton-on-Tees and paid for by the Bute family. The building materials were all shipped from Teesside. The sanctuary lamp is in the form of a ship's lamp. Stained-glass window by Fr Ninian Sloan of *Our Lady Star of the Sea* dedicated to the memory of the Royal and Allied navies stationed at Lossiemouth 1946–72 and donated by them.

- Sunday: 6.30pm
- Open by arrangement (01343 542280)

**MORAY**

## 94 OLD SEMINARY, SCALAN

### Scalan Pilgrimage Centre
### Braes of Glenlivet
### AB37 9JS

A NJ 246 195

Roman Catholic

⊕ www.scalan.co.uk

Turn off B9008 at Pole Inn

Scalan was a small, clandestine community set up in the Braes of Glenlivet for the training of Catholic priests. At this time, the practice of the Catholic religion was illegal and theoretically punishable by deportation. Scalan nevertheless remained in existence until 1799 and was finally closed by the Church itself when the repeal of the Penal Laws made it feasible to set up a larger and more visible seminary. Today, Scalan is a restoration project and a Pilgrimage Centre supported by the Scalan Association.

- Annual Mass, 1st Sunday in July, 4.00pm
- Open daily (01807 590340)

## 95 ST NINIAN'S CHURCH, TYNET

### Mill of Tynet
### AB56 5HH

A NJ 379 613

Roman Catholic

Linked with St Peter's Church, Buckie (67), St Mary's, Fochabers (84), St Gregory's Church, Preshome (97)

Just north of A98 at Bridge of Tynet, 4.5km (3 miles) north-east of Fochabers

The oldest post-Reformation Catholic church still in use in Scotland. At the request of the Duke of Gordon, 1755, built to resemble a sheep-cot in days when it was still an offence to celebrate Mass. Renovated 1957 by Ian Lindsay, architect, the long, low whitewashed building is still 'a church in disguise'.

- Sunday: 6.30pm
- Open by arrangement (01542 832196)

# PLUSCARDEN ABBEY

**Pluscarden
Elgin
IV30 8UA**

⚓ NJ 143 576

⛪ Roman Catholic

🌐 www.pluscardenabbey.org

8km (5 miles) south-west of Elgin

Founded in 1230 by Alexander II for Valliscaulian monks, it became Benedictine in 1454. Following the Reformation, it was the property of various local families, culminating in the Dukes of Fife, from whom it was bought by the Marquess of Bute, and whose son, Lord Colum, gave it to the monks in 1943. The buildings were eventually reoccupied in 1948. There are a number of interesting works of art, by prominent artists and architects following the restoration, including stained glass by Sadie McLellan. The Abbey offers retreat accommodation for men and women. Member of Moray Church trail.

- Sunday: 8.00am and 10.00am; weekdays: 9.00am
- Open daily 4.30am–8.30pm (01343 890257)

**MORAY**

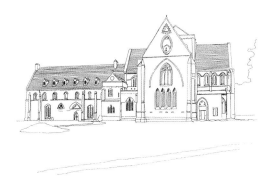

**97** ST GREGORY'S CHURCH, PRESHOME

**Preshome
AB56 5EP**

NJ 409 615

Roman Catholic

Linked with St Peter's Church, Buckie (67), St Mary's, Fochabers (84), St Ninian's Church, Tynet (95)

By Clochan. B9016, off A98

Built in 1788; wide rectangular church with harled walls and freestone dressing. The church is adorned with urn finials; its west end is a charming product of 18th-century taste, in which Italian Baroque has been skilfully naturalised to a Banffshire setting. Beautifully carved marble altar with gilded wooden reredos containing a copy of a painting of St Gregory the Great by Annibale Caracci. Two holy-water stoups of Portsoy marble. Exquisite stencilled wall decoration and coloured floor tiles in the chancel. Outstanding survival of pipe organ by James Bruce of Edinburgh, 1820, with carved Gothic case.

- Occasional services; check with St Peter's, Buckie
- Open by arrangement (01542 832196)

## 98 ROTHES PARISH CHURCH

**Seafield Square
Rothes
AB38 7AP**

⋀ NJ 278 492

🏠 Church of Scotland

Corner of High Street

Built in 1781; steeple added in 1870. A traditional Scottish design of the reformed tradition with the pulpit on the long wall, a three-sided gallery and an apse lit by large round-headed windows. Organ with pulpit in front.

- Sunday: 12.00 noon
- Open July and August, Tuesday to Thursday 2.00–4.00pm (01340 831381)

## 99 SPYNIE PARISH CHURCH

**Spynie
IV30 6XJ**

⋀ NJ 183 642

🏠 Church of Scotland

🌐 www.duffusparish.co.uk

Linked with Duffus Parish Church (76), Hopeman Parish Church (87)

Between Findrassie and Ardgilzean

Built in 1735 using dressed stone and belfry from the old church at Old Spynie. Traditional T-plan kirk with two galleries or lofts. Many of the pews are of the old box style originally allocated to heritors of the parish.

- See website for details
- Open by arrangement (01343 830276)

**MORAY**

## 100 CHURCH OF THE INCARNATION, TOMBAE

**Tombae
AB37 9JD**

NJ 217 257

Roman Catholic

http://stsylvesters.net

Linked with Sacred Heart, Aberlour (65), Our Lady of Perpetual Succour, Chapeltown (69), St Mary's, Dufftown (73), St Sylvester's, Elgin (81), St Columba's, Lossiemouth (93), St Michael's, Tomintoul (101)

1.5km (1 mile) south-east of Tomnavoulin

Designed by John Gall of Aberdeen, 1827–9, but completed in 1844 by Bishop James Kyle, replacing a simple 'mass-house' further upstream. The scenic rural site overlooks the River Livet, farmland and hills, now scantily populated. Gothic Revival church with pinnacled west front and lofty, elegant vaulted interior lit by large traceried windows. The former chancel served as the presbytery until 1862 when replaced by a neighbouring house, and then as a school until 1903.

- 9.30am every 3rd Sunday in rotation with Chapeltown and Tomintoul
- Open by arrangement (01343 542280)

## 101 ST MICHAEL'S, TOMINTOUL

**107 Main Street
Tomintoul
AB37 9EX**

NJ 169 185

Roman Catholic

http://stsylvesters.net

Linked with Sacred Heart, Aberlour (65), Our Lady of Perpetual Succour, Chapeltown (69), St Mary's, Dufftown (73), St Sylvester's, Elgin (81), St Columba's, Lossiemouth (93), Church of the Incarnation, Tombae (100)

At south end of Main Street

Built 1837 to a design by George Mathewson of Dundee, replacing a small chapel on the village outskirts. The cruciform church, lit by narrow Gothic windows, has a bellcote crowning the west gable. The east transept has been adapted as the presbytery. Interior remodelled 1930s and now largely decorated with artwork from adjoining St Michael's Youth Centre, a residential centre operated by the Diocese of Aberdeen in a former convent for those on retreat or visiting the Grampian Highlands.

- 9.30am every 3rd Sunday in rotation with Chapeltown and Tombae
- Open daily (01343 542280)

# Index

References are to each church's entry number in the gazetteer.